Jeremy Bamber

For those who help me hold it all together

Mum and Dad
The Saxton Brownes in all their forms (including the cats)
SALCK

Jeremy Bamber

Murder and Turmoil at White House Farm

Helen Saxton

An imprint of
Pen & Sword Books Ltd
Yorkshire - Philadelphia

First published in Great Britain in 2026 by
Pen & Sword True Crime
An imprint of
Pen & Sword Books Ltd
Yorkshire - Philadelphia

ISBN 978 1 03612 875 3

A CIP catalogue record for this book is available from the British Library.

Typeset in INDIA by IMPEC eSolutions
Printed and bound in England by CPI Group (UK) Ltd, Croydon, CRO 4YY

The Publisher's authorised representative in the EU for product safety is Authorised Rep Compliance Ltd., Ground Floor, 71 Lower Baggot Street, Dublin D02 P593, Ireland.
www.arccompliance.com

For a complete list of Pen & Sword titles please contact

PEN & SWORD BOOKS LIMITED
47 Church Street, Barnsley, South Yorkshire, S70 2AS, England
E-mail: enquiries@pen-and-sword.co.uk
Website: www.pen-and-sword.co.uk

or

PEN AND SWORD BOOKS
1950 Lawrence Rd, Havertown, PA 19083, USA
E-mail: uspen-and-sword@casematepublishers.com
Website: www.penandswordbooks.com

Contents

INTRODUCTION

Important Notice

On page 184, seven lines down from the top, this book says 'Matt Harris believes Jeremy Bamber is guilty'. This is a factual error and should read 'Matt Harris believes that Jeremy Bamber is innocent'.

Two Sides of the Same Coin

61-year-old June Bamber had been a secret war operative who now ran a successful farming business with her husband Nevill Bamber, also 61, who alongside his farming life was also a respected magistrate. Their adopted daughter, 27-year-old Sheila Caffell, was an aspiring model and a troubled, loving and fragile young woman. June, Nevill and Sheila died in 1985, alongside Sheila's six-year-old twin boys.

Whilst we know a fair amount about the personal lives of the adult victims involved in this horrific case, Daniel and Nicholas are all too often lumped together as 'the twins' or 'the boys' and by necessity will often be referred to as such in the following pages of this book. As with most tales of heinous murders, the perpetrator or accused inevitably becomes the sole, morbid focus from the moment the public become aware of their identity, and it is because of this that we must at least begin this tale by meeting Daniel and Nicholas before they become enveloped and lost in the story of their own deaths.

They were six years old at the time of their murder. Born in 1979, Daniel arrived a few minutes before his younger brother. These few minutes made all the difference to the dynamic between them, with Nicholas often referred to by those who knew him as the 'little brother' and played up to the role; let off the hook for mischievous behaviour by virtue of this label while Daniel stoically shouldered the responsibility of being the older, more sensible brother.

Like 'two sides of the same coin'[1] they developed similar yet very distinct personalities during their too-short lives. Daniel loved football and He-Man but also loved playing with the dolls traditionally, particularly in the 1970s, reserved for little girls. He nurtured everyone around him and was sensitive and empathetic to the feelings of those he loved, once professing his ambition to 'be a mummy'[2] one day despite ultimately understanding that this wasn't quite how the world worked, yet.

Daniel was creative, as was Nicholas, who had a particular affinity with nature and often created 'bright and colourful' artwork 'full of smiles and rainbows and fairies.'[3] He was much more aware of being his own person, unlike Daniel who 'didn't mind if people got them muddled up.'

Together though, they were greater than the sum of their parts. Inquisitive, outgoing, sociable and mischievous they took great delight in making people laugh whether by accident or design and perhaps because they were deeply embroiled in the creative and slightly alternative lifestyle of their father who, as an artist, numbered famous musicians among his family and friends, they were confident and at ease in the company of adults.

There are very few people alive now who knew the boys as well as their own father, Colin Caffell, from whose poignant memoir these memories and descriptions are borrowed. Colin himself is prone to being side-lined during discussions about this case. Even now, he is described by his former brother-in-law David Boutflour in a documentary made in 2021 not by name but as 'someone'[4] who Sheila had children with, reducing him to little more than a sperm donor. Perhaps this gives an unwitting insight in to how Colin was, or rather wasn't, welcomed into the bosom of the Bamber family. Despite this and although Colin did not die on 7 August 1985, in many ways he is as much a victim of the events as the people who did.

June, Nevill, Sheila, Daniel and Nicholas were all found dead in the early hours of 7 August 1985 at the Bamber's home, White House Farm in Tolleshunt D'Arcy, Essex, England. The police had been alerted a few hours earlier by Sheila's 24-year-old adopted brother Jeremy, following a claim that he had received a call from his father in which he was told 'your sister's gone berserk, and she's got a gun.'[5] The phone then went dead.

When the bodies were finally discovered around four hours later, at first, perhaps understandably, Sheila was believed to be the perpetrator of a tragic murder-suicide. However, following the discovery of further evidence implicating him in the crime, Jeremy Bamber was eventually convicted of all five murders and jailed in 1986 for a minimum of twenty-five years, which was later changed to a whole life tariff. Unless his ongoing campaign for appeal is successful, he will die in HMP Wakefield where, at the time of writing, he is held at His Majesty's pleasure.

For many people, the evidence which put Jeremy away is at best not compelling enough to warrant the guilty verdict he received and at worst fabricated, and therefore his conviction by a jury majority of ten to two is not just unsafe but represents a huge travesty of justice. Following several failed legal challenges and appeals he remains in prison still maintaining his innocence, adamant that he can prove that Sheila was to blame for the deaths of his family. He is not alone; he boasts a committed team of supporters campaigning on his behalf.

It is therefore important to not only recreate a timeline of events as evidenced by the accepted testimony at trial and the many witnesses to the family in the run up to that fateful night, but also to explain the reasons why his supporters believe he is innocent. Some are plausible, and some stretch the imagination but there is one thing for certain; his campaign team are nothing if not convinced of his innocence. As one podcaster explained, following an interview with some of his supporters 'they turned around and said to me that even if Jeremy were to admit his guilt, they would still have doubts over the conviction.'[6] Is this level of faith to be admired, or scorned?

Jeremy is certainly divisive; either he is 'evil, almost beyond belief'[7] per the words of the judge who sentenced him; a psychopathic family annihilator who is behind bars where he belongs, or the victim of one of Britain's longest running and most heinous miscarriages of justice. There is very little room for any other opinion.

Our thoughts about Sheila could be described as more complex. There are no two ways about it; she became a victim on 7 August 1985 no matter whether she pulled the trigger herself or whether she died at the hands of her brother. She was either murdered, or she was the victim of her own debilitating mental health issues over which she had little or no control.

And yet perhaps the reason why this case continues to be debated in the public arena is down to one simple truth. Due to the way in which Jeremy alerted police to his father's alleged phone call only two people could possibly have been responsible for this crime: Sheila or Jeremy. Either Jeremy is telling the truth, and Sheila shot her entire family before turning the gun on herself or he is lying, and he murdered all five of the people in White House Farm. If he was lying it was an audacious gamble on his part as his evidence put Sheila squarely in the frame. He left no possibility of an anonymous crazed gunman being blamed, or a deranged psychopath on the run or even the perpetrator of a burglary gone wrong. And if evidence were to emerge that Sheila could not possibly have been responsible, then he left himself open as the only other possible suspect.

If not Sheila Caffell, then Jeremy Bamber. If not Jeremy Bamber, then Sheila Caffell.

DESCENT

White House Farm

Murders occur all over the world in a myriad of different locations. They are perpetrated in homes, in woods, on pavements, in hospitals, schools and offices. They take place in parks, playgrounds and schools. While the act of murder is in itself universally abhorrent, often the circumstances and surroundings in which a particular murder occurs can shape how the public react to it, feel about it and henceforth view it in their minds' eye. The fact that these murders are often referred to by the name of the building in which they took place perhaps shows how iconic the building itself has become in the world of true crime. Not only did the farmhouse itself play no small part in the investigation and the subsequent campaigns and trials, but it has also since become in essence a gatekeeper of the truth within. What exactly went on in those rooms, within that silent, locked building on 7 August 1985? A cliché but nonetheless apt here; if these walls could talk, White House Farm would have an awful lot to tell us.

After the murders the farm became the subject of family arguments and resentment over ownership and perhaps the reason why it became so coveted by the family after the deaths of its household is because of its lineage within the Bamber family. This farm was not acquired with what is known as 'new money', a rather snobbish way to describe, for example, a recent acquisition by a lottery winner with a hankering for taste of rural life, but was a house which, by a series of oddly prophetic occurrences and deaths, made its way to becoming the home of June and Nevil Bamber in 1951, where they would reside for thirty-four years before their eventual deaths within it.

Those who are prone to superstition might be persuaded that White House Farm carries tragedy within it and that the events of 7

August 1985 were merely inevitable. Logically of course, a house made of bricks and mortar cannot hold any influence over what happens beneath its roof, but White House Farm's history is nonetheless compelling; with hindsight, it was at the very least beset by a series of interesting if not prescient coincidences.

Originally built in the early seventeenth century, by the mid-nineteenth century the impressive property in Tolleshunt D'Arcy was the residence of one Benjamin Page, who having lived there since birth, following his marriage to Elizabeth Seabrook in 1864 took over the running of it from his widowed mother. In 1887 his relative, Orbell Page, was found dead of a self-inflicted shotgun wound, just over a mile away from White House Farm. His death was deemed suicide by reason of temporary insanity; a seemingly cover-all explanation for any type of mental illness in the nineteenth century.

Whether or not this event had any lasting effect on Benjamin is difficult to tell, but he was by all accounts himself a man who was plagued by depression and, by 5 January 1892 he too would be dead by his own hand, having attempted to kill himself by ingesting poison on 29 December 1891. He was discovered by his daughter, retching and in extreme pain; she also found a spoon and the label from a bottle of poison nearby. He subsequently succumbed to its effects a few days later, following unsuccessful attempts by the local physician to save him. His death was ruled suicide while of unsound mind – similar, one imagines, to poor Orbell's temporary insanity.

Benjamin's widow, Elizabeth, stayed on and managed the farm with the help of their two sons, Frank and Hugh. When his mother died, Frank, as the eldest of the brothers, became the head of the farm but when Hugh died in 1950, Frank suffered a nervous breakdown although whether or not it was a result of his brother's death is difficult to tell. In November of the same year his body was found in a tank of water at the farm; it was first thought that he had drowned but when the subsequent inquest showed no signs of this being the cause, it was determined that the cold water had brought on a heart attack and that he was probably dead as he entered the water. Either way, the conclusion was that he had plunged into the water by his own free will and his death was also deemed to be the result of suicide. He was buried at St Nicholas's Church in Tolleshunt D'Arcy, where Benjamin and Orbell Page had also been laid to rest. It would eventually become the final resting place of June and Nevill Bamber, Sheila and Jeremy's adoptive parents.

June and Nevill's path to White House Farm ran via June's family; her father, Leslie Speakman married Mabel Bunting in 1919, and they lived in and ran Vaulty Manor Farm, a property just down the road from White House Farm, which Leslie co-managed with the unfortunate Frank Page. Following Frank's apparent suicide, Leslie approached his daughter June and his by then son-in-law Nevill to take up the tenancy of White House Farm and so, by 1951, they were established in their new home.

Nevill was by this time already working for Leslie at Vaulty, having first arrived in Essex in 1948, in a roundabout way at the behest of Robert Boutflour who would go on to become his brother-in-law. Robert's father, Professor Boutflour was a teacher at the Royal Agricultural College in Cirencester where Nevill attended as a student. When his son approached him to send helpers to work on the farm, he happily obliged with Nevill being one of those chosen.

Nevill got on famously with the Boutflours, and soon after he and June met, they started courting. Just one year later, June Speakman and Nevill Bamber were married on 3 September 1949 at St Peter's Church in Goldhanger. June's older sister, Pamela, was already married to the aforementioned Robert Boutflour and they would go on to have two children, David and Ann. Nevill's sister, Phyllis Speakman, married Reginald Pargeter and had two children, Anthony and Jacqueline. It would be a while though, before these two sets of cousins would meet the newest and youngest additions to their Aunty June and Uncle Nevill's family.

Nevill's father died in 1950, but his mother Beatrice lived until 1981 and in fact lived with the Bambers for a while, which was said to have a less than positive effect on June's mental health. June's father, Leslie, died in 1975, but her mother Mabel lived at Vaulty Manor until her death in 1986, tragically outliving her younger daughter. She would later unknowingly become the subject of contention following the murders, and the subsequent scrabbles for inheritance among her family.

The family arguments surrounding this inheritance can partly be understood simply by the sheer size of the estate which would eventually be bequeathed by June and Nevill. White House Farm was not the only property they owned, and while the rest play a less significant part in the events of 7 August 1985, they do add to the wider picture of what was at stake by the time June and Nevill died.

One such property and thriving business was known as the Osea Road Campsite, which was not only managed by Mabel but had been her brainchild and she proudly and successfully ran it until she was no longer able. Established in 1933 and situated on the land opposite Vaulty Manor where the family then lived, it started life as a convenient spot for local fruit pickers to pitch their tents while working. By all accounts Mabel was an astute businesswoman; she was aware of the growing trend in the United Kingdom for outdoor pursuits, and before long she found the site overwhelmed with visitors from all over the country but particularly from nearby London, perhaps with residents looking for somewhere rural enough to feel like a break from the big smoke yet close enough for easy travel. June and Pamela worked hard on the family business, and like her mother before her, June would go on to oversee the Osea Road site until her death, by which time she and Pamela each had a forty-two per cent interest in the park, with cousins Ann and Jeremy sharing the remaining sixteen per cent.

As with White House Farm itself, Osea Road would become inextricably linked with this saga, not least because it was yet another asset to argue over but also because it came up in the investigation and following trial having been the subject of a burglary not long before the murders which Jeremy admitted to being partially responsible for. At the time of writing, the site is now named Osea Leisure Park and appears to be a sprawling and successful holiday destination; the website is nostalgic for its beginnings, explaining;

> 'When Mabel Speakman opened her fields in 1933 to families of pea pickers it started a tradition and custom that endures to this day. After 80 years the values installed by Mabel are still alive at Osea today.'[1]

It has continued to stay in the family and at the time of writing is owned by Janie Robinson, Ann's daughter, who also turned nearby Vaulty Manor into a thriving wedding venue.

While his wife's focus lay with Osea Road, Leslie was busy running a total of six farms, Vaulty and three others very close by: Gardeners Farm, Charity Farm and White House Farm. Two others under his management, Burnt Ash Farm and Carbonells were situated in nearby Wix. Carbonells would go on to be the family home of Robert and Pamela Boutflour and their children, David and Ann; while technically still owned by Mabel Speakman, they paid her a nominal rent and it was still considered a part of the estate owned and handled by June's side of the family. Nevill however added his own significant weight to what went on to be the couple's legacy and property portfolio. His mother, Beatrice, owned Clifton House in Guildford, designed by her Arts and Crafts architect father and son's namesake, Ralph Bamber. It was an impressive home, large enough to be broken down and developed into several luxury flats by Nevill when he inherited the property after his mother's death.

While Nevill and June together went on to increase their property portfolio by the time they died, one purchase itself would add to the future animosity between Jeremy and his cousins. In November 1984, Nevill purchased the forty-eight-and-a-half-acre Little Renters Farm. He did so, it is said, following a cry for help from his niece, Ann, and her husband, Peter Eaton. The property had belonged to Peter's father and was passed down to Peter and his brother John when their father died. John planned to sell his share to property developers, but Peter was keen to keep the whole farm in the family. Nevill agreed to purchase Little Renters anonymously or at least without John discovering the identity of the buyer, following which the plan was for Ann and Peter to pay him back and therefore eventually own the farm outright.

Despite their flourishing businesses and otherwise outwardly successful life, June and Nevill were not blessed with children immediately following their marriage. Growing up, David, Ann, Anthony and Jacqueline all spent countless hours at White House Farm with their Uncle Nevill and Aunty June; in particular Anthony and Jaqueline, as their mother, Nevill's sister, had died in 1948 and with their father travelling frequently for work they often found themselves feeling rather rudderless. The cousins were said to consider White House Farm their second home, and, it might therefore be assumed, thought of June and Nevill as a set of surrogate parents. This predisposition to lovingly care for their wider family seems to have been passed down the generations; Mabel had taken on the care of her brother Jack's children in 1914 when his wife died; the children, Betty and Binks, would go on to become unofficial adopted sisters to June and Pamela and were also instrumental in the running of Osea Road.

It's therefore easy to see how the close knit yet somewhat complicated family was formed, and even easier to understand why June and Nevill's subsequent struggle to have children could have seemed all the more unfair and devastating to them, given the abundant love they apparently had to give.

Phyllis and Jeremy

It is often easy, but certainly unfair, to view murder victims as two dimensional; something which is almost never applied to the perpetrators or alleged perpetrators. For them, their behaviour tends to be openly analysed with every word and movement studied in minute detail to the point where the public believe that they know them personally while their victims often remain as real to them only as their last snapshot.

Nevill and June Bamber are no different. On the surface they appear to be a hard-working yet arguably privileged couple building a traditional farming life for themselves in rural Essex. However, the idyllic and perhaps routine and mundane existence which is often portrayed as simply beginning with their courtship and marriage and continuing from there could not be further from the truth.

Nevill was by all accounts a charming, handsome and athletic man, coming from a lineage of high-ranking serving officers in the armed forces. He himself went on to join the RAF and was called up in 1941, going on to take part in daring night raids in North Africa amongst many other locations. After being shot down in action he took a while to recuperate, during which he completed a brief stint in Egypt following which he was eventually demobbed in September 1947. It was then that he joined the Royal College of Agriculture in Cirencester, from where he was summoned by Robert Boutflour and ended up in Essex.

June was also no stranger to action during the war and her activities remain alluringly secretive with scant details remaining. However, it is known that she was a member of Churchill's secret army, something of which even her closest family were unaware at the time.

It appears that she joined the First Aid Nursing Yeomanry (FANY) and through this was enlisted into its affiliated partner, the Special Operations Executive (SOE). As a result of this she was interviewed by MI5, signed the Official Secrets Act, underwent intensive wireless and security training and eventually learned to parachute and fully embodied the role of a skilled agent. It's known that she was equally if not more travelled than her future husband, with stints in India and the Far East. Following Japan's formal surrender on 2 September 1945 her group began to disband, and she was officially demobbed in February 1946 and back at Vaulty Manor in time to coincide with her future husband's arrival in 1948.

What would come to light later are tales of mental health anguish, zealous religious ideas and desperate family struggles. One likes to imagine though that the memory of the exhilaration these two individuals must have felt during their service would at least have had a lasting effect on their outlook in life. While in no way glorifying war and the stress and trauma which inevitably accompany one's involvement in it, Nevill and June must have experienced more excitement and drama before they even met each other than many of us live through in a lifetime and it is hard to imagine that they would not at least sometimes look back with pride at their achievements. While their lives did not start from the point at which they married, it's perhaps little wonder their dream was to then settle to a quiet life on the farm with the prospect of children and grandchildren to look forward to.

Sadly, although they were surrounded by prosperous relatives and flourishing businesses, this was the one thing they really craved, and which proved elusive. Events might later go on to suggest that this craving was rather the pursuit of the traditional idea of a picture-perfect family rather than any particular maternal or paternal instincts, but this of course could be said of many people in the 1950s, an era when it was the 'done thing' to get married and have children and indeed frowned upon if this path was not taken.

It is perhaps unfair, though, to make assumptions of this kind; the couple realised soon enough that they were unable to conceive naturally and no matter their motivation, those of us who have not experienced it cannot imagine how frustrating and heart-breaking it must have been for Nevill and in particular June to be subjected to this in the days before the options of IVF and surrogacy were open and readily available to them. Perhaps even more soul destroying though, was of course that June was experiencing this in the days when women were negatively defined by their inability to conceive and give birth, and indeed going one step further with the burden of blame falling on them even if it were to be proven that the root of the infertility was their male partner. Family lore suggest that this was indeed the case, with the suggestion that it was Nevill who was suffering from infertility issues. Given this level of pressure that both they themselves and society had heaped on them it's no surprise that during the six years when they tried and failed to conceive, June suffered from the first of many nervous breakdowns. By the time the couple were in their mid-thirties and June had to undergo an operation to have an ovarian cyst removed, all hope of conceiving naturally was effectively gone.

And so it was that in 1957 the couple adopted their first child from the Church of England Children's Society; a baby girl whom they called Sheila Jean. Sheila was the daughter of an eighteen-year-old named Christine, the unmarried daughter of a senior chaplain to the Archbishop of Canterbury who, perhaps unsurprisingly, was unwilling to allow his daughter to keep her baby. In true 1950s' style, the unwed pregnant teenager was sent away on some pretence and when it was all over returned to the family home, re-joining her siblings who were all absolutely oblivious to the fact that they now had a niece. Christine had named her baby Phyllis. Unbelievably, Phyllis, later Sheila, found her way to the Bambers not through chance but through design; her grandfather, the aforementioned chaplain, had met Nevill during the war and 'selected the Bamber family from a small number of suitable households'[1] as the place in which his granddaughter should live from thereon in, effectively choosing a person he had fleetingly worked with in the war as a suitable parental substitute for his daughter, the baby's own mother.

Despite the fact that in the past June had, on two separate occasions, suffered mental breakdowns severe enough to require hospitalisation, the second of which was triggered by the adoption of their daughter, Nevill and June applied to adopt a second baby in 1960, again from the Church of England Society, and were accepted. In 1961, they adopted a baby boy, whom they named Jeremy Nevill.

Jeremy's birth story originated from a slightly different place than Sheila's; he was conceived through an affair between a married man and his mistress. This in itself is not that unusual but what followed is less common, and yet potentially heart breaking in later life for the baby who was given away, should they ever find out the truth. Jeremy's birth father eventually divorced his wife and he and his birth mother went on to marry and have two more children, Jeremy's full siblings. While Sheila eventually met her birth mother and began the emotional process of bonding, despite Jeremy's birth parents keeping in touch with the Bambers for a few years, no attempt was ever made by them to reconcile with their first-born child, nor by him to meet them.

Growing up in their particular family dynamic appears not to have been easy for Sheila and Jeremy; family members recall June and Nevill's lack of discipline with the two, stemming from an insecurity that they might be taken away from them at any moment. Anthony and Jacqueline, their older cousins, were treated almost as their own children by June and Nevill, and the two adopted siblings were apparently apt to feel a little unloved by their parents in their presence. It seems that June absolutely loved her children but was unable to show them affection. This was often expressed later in life through money by offering to buy houses and businesses for her children to try and solve problems which might have been better dealt with through love and care. This was evidenced perhaps by Sheila lamenting that 'her parents gave her everything she needed apart from physical affection.'[2] When they were young, Jeremy is described as the more placid of the two, with Sheila being sensitive, spirited, and with a quick temper. However, Sheila was also tactile, loving and spontaneous whereas Jeremy apparently grew to be 'snooty'[3] and then showed himself to be 'a real wimp'[4] when his classmates teased him about it although this does seem a slightly harsh description to level at a child.

The Bamber children both started their educational journey at their local primary school but were later moved to Malden Court, a nearby preparatory school. When Sheila was 10 years old, she was enrolled in Moira House, a boarding school situated in Sussex, more than one hundred miles away from home where she was said to be deeply unhappy. However, in 1970 after moving to Old Hall School in Hethersett, an alternative boarding school in Norfolk, she became much more settled. On completing her education there in 1974, June and Nevill enrolled her on a secretarial course at an expensive finishing school, St Godrick's Secretarial College, which took her to London, and while he was living here that she would go on to meet her future husband, Colin Caffell.

Concurrently, in 1970 when Jeremy was nine, he was sent to board at Gresham's, another school in Norfolk where, on learning that he was adopted, his classmates reportedly gave him the unsavoury nickname of the 'bastard' against a background of snobbery and class divide. It was while a pupil here that some sources claim Jeremy was sexually abused although the details are sketchy; one source was his future brother-in-law Colin Caffell, who said that Jeremy was 'emotionally, physically and, according to Jeremy sexually abused by the older boys'[5] although Jeremy himself doesn't appear to have officially confirmed this.

By the time Sheila had moved to London, Jeremy was moving up to the senior school at Gresham's and continued his studies there, despite being destined to eventually take over the running of White House Farm from his father. Jeremy's feelings on this matter are diversely reported; he said he knew that it was his destiny and was aware 'from a young age that I'd be a farmer'[6] and asserted that he was in fact quite at peace and on board with this plan. Nevill's secretary, Barbara Wilson, however, recalled otherwise and later reported the dissatisfaction he expressed with the course his life was taking. Her interpretation was that Jeremy came from a 'moneyed family' and therefore didn't feel he had to work, which sometimes caused 'fierce' arguments with his father who, she said, 'made her promise that she would look after the farm if anything was to happen to him'[7] not long before he was killed.

By 1977 Jeremy was certainly beginning to rebel, smoking cannabis and sneaking out of the school grounds to check out live bands. He moved into sixth form to study his O-Levels but wasn't particularly popular and reportedly liked to wind other pupils up, described by his headmaster William Thomas as 'a disruptive influence' who went on to declare that 'I had come to know him as a boy you could not trust.'[8] Perhaps tellingly, given what was to come, he also described him as 'somewhat of a boaster with regard to his financial potential.'

However, in what seems to have been a bit of a turning point for Jeremy, in 1978, while studying for his A-Levels at Gresham's, he decided he'd had enough of boarding school and persuaded his parents to allow him to continue his studies back home at the Colchester Institute, where he went on to study Biology and Mathematics. Perhaps on being released from boarding school and the snobbery which surrounded it he now finally found his tribe, as he would later be described during this period as gentle and pleasant, someone who got on with everyone and who was 'popular with the girls.'[9]

The Devil's Child

And so, Sheila and Jeremy were forging very different paths in life. It was expected that Jeremy would follow in his parents' footsteps both on the farm and at Osea Road but there doesn't ever seem to have been a suggestion that Sheila would do so. Given the social background of the late 1970s, this might at first glance look to have been due to stereotypical gender bias. However, given her mother's background and the history of strong and shrewd businesswomen in the family it seems unlikely that this was strictly down to any kind of misogyny or belief that running a business was not 'women's work.'

It's more likely, then, that this lack of expectation was due to Sheila's disinterest and potential ineptitude in the world of business. This is not to be unkind; even in the words of someone who loved and knew her best, she was 'a girl who loved to talk even if, half the time, she didn't understand what she or anyone else was talking about.'[1] Less a criticism and more an observation that she was not cut out for business and, more pertinently, had no desire to be. And this person who loved her, his words recalling his initial adoration of Sheila, turned out to be her future husband, Colin Caffell.

While still a student at the secretarial college and during a night out with friends, Sheila and Colin met in a local pub, and according to him they were mutually hooked before long. Colin was 21 years old, and Sheila was just 17 and an aspiring model; she possessed the striking and dreamy 1970s style beauty required for success in this field but was ultimately not cut out for a career in modelling. Perhaps now with the domination of reality television and social media, society is far more aware of the unlikelihood of fulfilling one's dream of becoming a model and the brutal reality of modelling life even if successful; it is a far stretch from the world we may have erroneously imagined in the past, an 'easy' job where swanning around looking good was all it took to make it big. The modelling industry notoriously chews girls up and spits them out and while Sheila's failure to make the big time didn't happen in such a dramatic fashion, it seems likely that the guileless, trusting, enthusiastic, innocent and naïve child of which Colin Caffell paints a picture was simply not resilient enough for this world.

Nevertheless, as their relationship progressed, Colin recalled that he and Bambs, as became his affectionate nickname for Sheila, due to her surname and, her fragility and vulnerability, were blissfully happy, albeit living in poverty. Sheila pursued her modelling career having dropped out of secretarial school due to a total lack of interest in the course on her part. She also attempted a brief stint as a trainee hairdresser while Colin continued his studies at Camberwell School of Art. Young as they were, Sheila fell pregnant in 1975 and once they had come to terms with the idea, they both intended to keep the baby and perhaps get married. June, however, had other ideas. She insisted upon, or rather coerced her daughter into the idea that an abortion was the most sensible if not the only prudent course of action, and Sheila grudgingly agreed.

It was not long after this when an event took place which is widely credited as deeply harming Sheila's already fragile mental health and which was the catalyst of a lifelong conflict between mother and daughter, embroiling them in a hell of mental health anguish and religious mania. June was an overtly religious woman; Barbara Wilson recalled post-it notes dotted around the place with verses from the Bible written on them, and that June was apt to 'quote the Bible at you'[2] if she thought people weren't 'doing things correctly.'

It was all precipitated by a rather innocuous if perhaps inappropriate decision by the young couple during a visit by Colin to White House

Farm following the abortion, to comfort Sheila. In his words, they 'decided to strip off completely and sunbathe naked'[3] while out picnicking in the surrounding fields. They made the most of the beautiful summer's day and while of course it would be disingenuous to suggest that there was nothing in any way sexual about this it was by no means the motivation behind it; they were trying to put behind them the trauma of an unwanted abortion and move forward, revelling in their love for each other. Given what Sheila had recently been through this was not a physical connection; they talked, Colin said, for an hour or so about the decision while enjoying the sun. With Sheila anxious and Colin attempting to comfort her, they were discovered by an incandescent June who had been driving across the fields in her Mini looking for the pair and who then branded their behaviour 'disgusting.'[4]

Later, back at the house, during a dressing down by June which Colin would later recall as 'emotionally catastrophic'[5] for her, June branded her daughter 'the Devil's child'[6] for her behaviour in the fields. While one might be forgiven for thinking that Colin might be too close to the situation to be impartial, he was not the only person who was aware of the devastating effect these words had on Sheila. Several of her friends went on to describe the deeply negative emotional effect it had on her and the exchange was even referred to by her psychiatrist during the subsequent trial as the phrase 'on which she hung her psychosis.'[7]

The complexities of mental illness could fill a book in themselves, but despite not being blood related it is curious how June and Sheila shared quite similar mental health issues. Throughout her life, June suffered from numerous bouts of depression, and more than one nervous breakdown, the second of which was seemingly triggered by Sheila's adoption and during which she was admitted into a private psychiatric clinic in Northampton in 1958. While he didn't go on to treat June until 1982, Dr Hugh Ferguson, a consultant psychiatrist at the clinic since 1978, looked back on her initial diagnosis and speculated that her depression was 'somewhat religiose, disturbed thoughts as well as disturbed feelings. That's the difference between a clinical depression and a psychotic depression – there's a breaking with reality.'[8] Following her lack of response to medication, the choice of treatment was then electroshock therapy which, if controversial did seem to prove effective.

Sheila's mental health issues might have been exacerbated by her feelings and tumultuous guilt surrounding pregnancy and abortion, but they were also inextricably linked to her relationship with her mother, with Sheila confessing to dwelling on 'thoughts of God and the Devil' and that she was 'caught up in a coven of evil'[9] with June. It was in 1983 when she began to hear voices telling her that she was, for example Joan of Arc or the Virgin Mary. She was referred to Dr Ferguson who was by then also treating June, and who described Sheila at this stage as delusional and psychotic. Despite her fractious relationship with June, Dr Ferguson was convinced this merely exacerbated Sheila's feelings particularly when she was eventually diagnosed with schizophrenia in 1985; in his opinion while she certainly didn't help, June was not the cause of her daughter's illness. By the time of her death, Sheila was on regular injections of anti-psychotic medication, Haloperidol. She was prone to forgetting to take her medication, and this method helped to ensure continuity.

In 1977, Sheila fell pregnant again and this time, determined to make it work, the couple decided to get married and did so on 14 May that year. At the insistence of her mother the ceremony took place at Chelmsford Registry Office and the bride dressed in off-white, June having forbidden a white wedding in her local church for fear of the embarrassment this hypocrisy would cause her. For Colin and Sheila, despite their love for each other, the marriage had been the result of what could be perceived as a bribe, as June had offered to buy the couple a flat in London if they went through with the marriage for appearance's sake. Tragically, in what Sheila apparently thought of as 'divine retribution'[10] for her previous abortion, she suffered a miscarriage later that year.

Now living in a flat in Hampstead gifted by June and with Colin feeling grudgingly beholden to his parents-in-law, Sheila went to Japan for a modelling assignment which failed to live up to expectations. During her time there she worked incredibly long hours, and it was a place where models were treated as 'little more than prostitutes'[11] and so it seemed to mark the beginning of the end for her career. On her return, she became pregnant again and tragically, miscarried for a second time. It can be easy sometimes to forget how young Sheila and Colin were during this tumultuous period but here was a vulnerable young girl who, before she had reached the age of 21 had married and suffered one unwanted abortion and two miscarriages. Not only that, but her relationship with Colin was beginning to deteriorate, not altogether unsurprisingly given the mix of mental illness, miscarriages and the interference of overbearing parents. Heartbreakingly, it was during Sheila's twenty-first birthday party at their flat that Colin disappeared for a few hours, leaving her distraught and angry. It later transpired that he had been with another woman; the person he would eventually leave her for.

Despite this, Sheila found herself pregnant again in 1978, and this time, with twins.

Turmoil

In the meantime, Jeremy was enjoying his own forays into the world of adult relationships. Having failed his A-Levels he decided against retaking them and instead floated around aimlessly for a while before deciding to head to Australia and New Zealand, staying for around a year during which he developed a passion for diving. Far from wanting to follow in his father's footsteps as he had once claimed was his destiny, it seems that his dream now was to forge a career in this area, perhaps with a long-term plan to return to the Southern Hemisphere to live out this idyllic dream.

However, he returned to the UK in 1981 where, according to family and friends, he became slightly more active in the local community than he had been when younger. Having been sent to boarding school at a fairly young age neither he nor his sister had been able to welcome the chance to forge many meaningful relationships with local peers, and subsequently had gained a reputation as being rather aloof and, one could speculate, may have been rather lonely living in the no-mans-land between a school where they did not feel they fitted in and their home ground where they were not encouraged to mix with the locals. Barbara Wilson recalled that although Nevill and June were 'like the landlords of the village really',[1] Sheila and Jeremy never really fitted in with village life. They were, she said, a 'different class' of people and felt they had the right to use their parents' money. Indeed, as the one who often wrote the cheques, she confirms that 'most of the money went to Jeremy and Sheila', particularly when Jeremy 'got into difficulties.'

However, Jeremy at least seemed keen to overcome this lack of social cohesion and, perhaps due to his earlier transfer back to the local college, he found himself starting to finally fit in. It was by entering the Goldhanger social scene that he met his first serious girlfriend, Suzette, or Sue, Ford. In an echo of his sister's choice of partner who was perhaps a less than suitable match in the eyes of their parents, Jeremy's chosen partner was a married woman in her early thirties with three children.

While it might seem that Jeremy was gifted more freedom than his fragile sister (it seems highly unlikely, for example, that June and Nevill would have allowed Sheila to travel to Australia unaccompanied before she was married) he nonetheless seemed aware that this relationship would be frowned upon by his parents and initially kept it a secret. He was right, of course. When the relationship eventually became known to his parents his father, he said, initially liked Sue but his mother 'was not impressed'.[2] Later, however, his father came to agree with his wife and when Jeremy went so far as to move in with Sue, Nevill threatened to disinherit him unless he called off the relationship. Eventually they did split for a short while, during which Jeremy had a brief liaison with a girl named Jane, following which he reconciled briefly with Sue. Jeremy might have enjoyed more freedom in his social life than his sister, but he was not totally immune to his mother's overbearing and controlling nature when it came to her children's relationships.

It was during his involvement with Sue, which at one point allegedly became so serious that it involved a proposal of marriage, that Jeremy seemed to form his first local friendships, some of which would go on to play rather a major part in the murder enquiry and his subsequent arrest. Malcolm Waters and Michael Deckers were fairly prominent in this circle of friends, not least because they were business partners who ran the local pub and meeting place the Frog & Bucket, where it is said they allowed Jeremy to drink for free, in return for potatoes from the farm which they happily accepted in lieu of monetary payment. Here he also met Malcolm's girlfriend, Liz Rimmington.

Another friend who, unbeknownst to him went on to become a key figure in the investigation, was Matthew Macdonald who became drawn into the group through his attraction to Sue's friend, Christine Bacon, who had recently separated from her husband. However, it turned out that it was a drunken one-night fling between Matthew and Sue, which they both claimed was not sexual in nature that had caused that first brief split between Sue and Jeremy. Matthew, despite his pursuit and eventual affair with Christine and flirtation with Sue, was married. While the group might have displayed a fairly casual attitude to marriage, it must be remembered that this was a group of young adults in their very early twenties and their behaviour might well be seen as something of a warning against leaping into marriage at such a young age. Despite the liberation of the swinging sixties, the very British hangover of 'no sex before marriage' was perhaps somewhat to blame for this and the inevitable dissatisfaction some couples must have felt with the life they were now living, which their choices had left them with.

Perhaps because of the turbulent nature of Sue and Jeremy's relationship, by August 1982 he was headed to New Zealand again, this time with five thousand pounds in his pocket, funds given to him by his father to enable him to undertake a comprehensive scuba diving course. It was during this visit that he met yet another figure who would go on to play a part in the investigation later. Brett Collins was a native New Zealander and on meeting Jeremy they immediately became firm friends. Brett, he said, 'liked the look of [Jeremy]' as he had an 'air of royalty about him.'[3] While it has no bearing at all on whether or not Jeremy is guilty of murder, it has been implied that Brett and Jeremy's relationship may have been more than platonic, a fact which Brett, who is bisexual, corroborated in future interviews but which Jeremy pointedly did not. No matter what the nature of their relationship there is no doubt that they became very good friends; Brett would be a huge support to Jeremy following the murders and even find himself arrested alongside him at one stage.

Jeremy was still technically in a relationship with Sue during his trip abroad and, by her account, their relationship may well have stood the test of time had it not been for outside influences. She even said that the couple were desperate for a child, but she tragically suffered three miscarriages during their stormy relationship. However, not long after Jeremy's return to England their relationship began to peter out and eventually it officially ended. Unofficially however their sexual relationship continued sporadically even after he had entered his next serious and, from every conceivable viewpoint, most significant relationship.

By 1983, Malcolm and Michael had sold the Frog & Bucket and were now the owners of a pizza restaurant called Sloppy Joes where Liz Rimmington was the manager, their friend Julie Mugford had recently been employed as a waitress and where Jeremy worked behind the bar most evenings. Julie was 19 years old and a student at Goldsmiths in London studying for a degree in education and shared a house in Lewisham with a friend called Susan Battersby. She and Jeremy inevitably met at work and enjoyed their first date, rather unusually, on Boxing Day of that year. Jeremy, Julie said, 'swept me off my feet'.[4]

By the time they met Jeremy was settled into his own cottage in Goldhanger and working full time for his father on the farm during the day, but while his route to this relatively stable existence was smooth it wasn't without issues for some of the other people involved. Earlier in 1983, perhaps in an attempt to help their son to settle down, Nevill and June offered Jeremy a permanent position at the farm which came with it his own house, Bourtree Cottage. With that, Jeremy moved out of White House Farm and into a shared house with Michael, Liz and Malcolm as a stepping stone to Bourtree cottage, which was owned by his parents but at that time occupied by Kate Foakes. Her two sons, Len and David Foakes, both worked for the Bambers at White House Farm. David, however, was soon made redundant, following which his mother Kate was given six months' notice to leave the cottage, hence the need for Jeremy to house share for a while, waiting for it to become available for him to move in to.

1984 was a tumultuous year for Jeremy, particularly in regard to his love life. He was unfaithful to Julie not only with his former girlfriend Sue but with Julie's friend Liz and had previously enjoyed a fling with a woman called Virginia Greaves. More worryingly, he had a one-night stand with another, unnamed friend of Julie's which was 'witnessed' by another friend of Jeremy's, Charles Marsden. Charles also later recalled Jeremy having 'lots of girlfriends and one-night stands' during his and Julie's relationship. The one-night stand was worrying because it allegedly appears to have been a date rape. Charles alleges that the girl was very drunk when she, himself and Jeremy ended up at Bourtree Cottage following an evening in the pub and that he woke up to find Jeremy having sex with the girl or, more shockingly that she herself recalled that she suddenly found him 'on top of me having intercourse.' This left her feeling 'shocked, angry and abused'[5] and wondering if she had been drugged. According to some sources, the friend told Julie about the incident, presumably in the hopes that she would see Jeremy's true colours. However, it appears that Jeremy talked her round and Julie, either through naivety on her part, or manipulation on his, took Jeremy at his word and broke contact with her friend.

Not only was Jeremy's love life fairly turbulent at this point, but both he and Julie were allegedly dabbling in various illegal activities. Jeremy was apparently growing cannabis at Bourtree Cottage and dealing it locally, and Julie and her flatmate Susan also found themselves in trouble following an incident which was brought up during her later testimony in court. She and Susan decided to report Susan's cheque book as missing, and then used it to make thousands of pounds worth of purchases. On discovering what they'd done, Jeremy apparently laughed and chided them for being naughty, following which they apparently felt so guilty that they gave the spoils of their cheque fraud away. By 1985, moving on from the light cannabis dealing, Jeremy and by association Julie, also found themselves committing burglary at the family caravan park, Osea Road. The theft was allegedly Jeremy's idea in order to bring to his mother's attention the lack of security he claimed to have alerted her to; Julie faithfully kept watch while Jeremy broke in, staged a crime scene and stole around nine hundred pounds in cash.

Meanwhile, Sheila herself was experiencing huge upheavals of her own. In 1979 she gave birth to twin boys, Daniel and Nicholas. Given how desperate she had become to have children by this time, one might imagine the days and weeks surrounding their birth were some of the happiest times of her life. However, it seems that Colin had already mentally checked out of the marriage by then and indeed was having a full-blown affair with 18-year-old Jan Flowers, daughter of prolific bass player Herbie Flowers, and the girl he had absconded with during Sheila's twenty-first birthday party. By the time of Sheila's death, however, Jan and Colin had split up and he was with a new partner, Heather. Despite this massive upheaval at such a vulnerable time, Colin never turned his back on his duties as a parent and remained a staunch support and advocate for Sheila right up until she died and, of course, afterwards. Sheila understandably took the break-up badly but had already struggled with the difficulties of parenthood. While it certainly would have contributed significantly, her marriage break-up and husband's infidelity were by no means the sole cause of her subsequent struggles to care for the boys.

Sheila's mental health had been a major concern for a while, but it now became so debilitating that she was unable to hold down a job. Following a cry for help when she contacted Camden social services in fear that she would harm her children, the boys were now under the care of social services and while they were never taken away from her, they were sent out for daily fostering, essentially a type of daytime childcare and respite for Sheila. Several incidents are cited as a cause for concern about Sheila's parenting; Daniel had once prompted a health worker to worry when she saw a burn on his cheek, knee and stomach which was subsequently deemed to be accidental. The concern was more over Sheila's lack of urgency in getting him the required medical help than that she had potentially caused the injury itself. Another time Nicholas was involved in a minor accident when he fell out of a taxi he had been travelling in with his mother and brother, apparently following yet another turbulent visit to White House Farm. While it's unclear exactly what happened, there was never any implication that it was anything other than accidental, but Sheila later admitted that she was not really concentrating on the boys, with her mother's 'religious rantings'[6] still ringing in her ears from earlier.

Following their daughter's divorce, Nevill and June appeared to exert even more control over Sheila. They were now essentially in charge of her well-being and oversaw her medication, something which Sheila struggled with, continuing to turn to Colin by default to fight her corner. Her parents sold the Hampstead flat she had shared with him and instead bought her a flat in Maida Vale and so it was that by July 1982 Sheila was living there alone with the twins. Between then and her eventual death her life was marked by ups and downs but settled into somewhat of a routine.

It was during this time that her mental health issues spiralled but she and Colin between them successfully parented the twins, with Colin understandably doing the lion's share of the care. The boys stayed with him every weekend and sometimes during the week and he absolutely adored and relished this time he had with them. By 1982 social services closed the case on Daniel and Nicholas who went on to attend nursery and then school. Sheila attempted to work, with a brief stint as a cleaner. While it might be easy to remember Sheila only in terms of the negative aspects of her life which were, admittedly numerous, she was often seen to be in good spirits; she had become very friendly with Tora Tomkinson, the mother of a child at the twins' nursery and would socialise with the children and occasionally visit the local wine bar. She had also developed a relationship with Iranian born Farhad Emami, known as Freddie, who always maintained that their relationship was platonic; no matter whether this is true, he remained a support to Sheila right up until her death. It was with his help that Sheila decided to track down and ultimately meet her birth mother, Christine which started to bring her some joy and closure.

While Sheila loved her father and relished his visits, she was less enthusiastic about contact with her mother which inevitably revolved around being told how to parent the boys, how to manage her mental health and generally exuded negativity. While Jeremy was apparently proud of his sister, albeit perhaps envious of her London lifestyle, he visited and socialised, but it seems that his and his parents' attitude to her by this time, and particularly following her diagnosis in 1983, was one of bewilderment. 'We never discussed it as a family and so were all ignorant of the "hows and wherefores" of schizophrenia' he said, and even admitted that his opinion of Sheila, allegedly shared by the family, was that she was 'going bonkers.'[7]

MURDER

I Didn't Mean to be Horrible to Jeremy

As an indication of the way in which Colin and Sheila dealt with their break-up, Colin threw a housewarming party for this new flat on Saturday 3 August 1985 to which he not only invited Sheila, but also actively encouraged her to become involved in the planning of it along with Daniel and Nicholas who, he recalled fondly, loved entertaining. She arrived early to help prepare, a moment in their lives which Colin described as 'lovely, just the four of us'[1] working together to get everything ready for the party. At the time, this seemed to prove they were making co-parenting work for everyone involved and in particular for the benefit of their sons.

Colin appears to have generally got along with Jeremy during his marriage to Sheila, and as such Jeremy and Julie were also quite naturally invited to the party. However, Colin recalled that when he asked her to extend the invitation Sheila seemed reluctant to phone her brother. Rather than a sinister foreshadowing of what was to come, this reaction, Colin felt, was instead partly her 'beginning to display those familiar long periods of becoming distant and vague again.'[2] The party was a success, although Sheila was not at her best. Despite, or perhaps because of the former rekindling of the family unit while just the four of them prepared the party, Colin recalled that, in hindsight, Sheila may well have hoped that this was a precursor to them getting back together and that she seemed crushed on meeting his newest girlfriend, Heather, at the party.

Sheila was withdrawn and had little to do with her brother throughout the evening and shortly after midnight she asked Colin to take her home. This action makes it very clear that Sheila still very much relied on her ex-husband in so many ways and treated him at least on a practical level almost as though they were still married. Colin, however, had been drinking and suggested Jeremy could take her home instead. The suggestion made her appear nervous, if not a little frightened. In an echo of when she had been reluctant to personally invite Jeremy to the party in the first place, she asked Colin to do the asking. Colin obliged, and Jeremy duly took her home.

Nobody but Jeremy and Sheila could possibly know the topic of the conversation that took place during the car journey but on his return to the party talk turned to Sheila's treatment and developed into a long chat which made Colin feel uncomfortable. He had, he said, an unnerving feeling that Jeremy was 'stirring' things. Sheila had previously confided in Colin that she was unhappy with the treatment and medication path she was on, but her parents said they knew best and had faith that the current treatment was fine. This angered Colin, so Jeremy's following assertion during their chat that night that his parents had no respect for Colin and 'treated him like dirt'[3] understandably rankled. Jeremy opined that they had been 'bludgeoned into marriage'[4] by his parents and that now he and Julie were getting the same treatment. Furthermore, he described Sheila as being a 'difficult and selfish person' and suggested that Colin had been forced to look after the boys as she was 'incapable' and that he saw the twins as a millstone around Colin's neck, apparently assuming that Colin also felt this way about his own children. He did not.

The following day, Sunday 4 August 1985, Colin picked Sheila up from her Maida Vale flat at around 4.00 pm in his Volkswagen camper van and, along with Daniel and Nicholas, they headed to White House Farm to allow June and Nevill to help Sheila care for their grandchildren while Colin and Heather went on a trip to Norway. In the same way that Jeremy would later be the only living person able to report the events on the night of the murders, Colin is the only living person who can describe the actions, atmosphere and context of what happened on 4 August, and his account is compelling and somewhat prophetic.

Sheila said very little during the journey, and was very quiet, even for her. The boys however were reliving the excitement of the previous night's party, but Daniel, as the more sensitive of the two boys, was showing some trepidation about the forthcoming visit, a feeling which was shared by his father. Colin put his own trepidation down to a mixture of June's religious excesses which he knew made the boys feel uncomfortable – they had already asked their father to have a word with June when he dropped them off about the 'constant kneeling to pray'[5] when they visited - and Sheila's mental health which always deteriorated whenever she spent time with her mother. He went so far as to say that he had a gut feeling that they shouldn't go which could be put down to hindsight, but it could also have been a very genuine feeling that something sinister was about to happen over the coming days. Conversely, it could also be interpreted that he knew that Sheila was on a knife edge, and that he subconsciously thought she might do something regrettable.

Daniel had recently decided to become vegetarian, and he had also asked Colin to speak to June about shouting at them if they didn't eat their meat, something which she was prone to do, and which understandably upset them. It's heart-breaking to feel that two small children should feel the need for such prerequisites when visiting their grandparents, but Colin, who always advocated for his sons' rights to be treated individually and with respect did so and recalled that 'June was having a very hard time not retaliating'[6] to his request. To add fuel to the fire, Nevill started teasing Daniel about not eating meat, warning him that he'd never be a farmer if he didn't, following which Colin reiterated to his former parents-in-law that they must respect Daniel's wishes.

Despite his advocacy for his children perhaps causing a little tension within the group Colin stayed for supper and indeed was invited to stay the night but he chose instead to leave and head back to his own home. This decision, he recalls, left not only Sheila disappointed, but he in himself for failing to stick up for her as much as he could or perhaps should have. He described the last physical contact he would ever have with his children as 'the most desperately strong embrace that I can ever remember them giving me'[7] as he left them at White House Farm, knowing that they were both feeling deeply insecure about the visit ahead.

Over the next couple of days, several people came into contact with Sheila, both at the farm and during visits with her mother and each describe varying behaviours belying her state of mind, as perceived by them, during the period of time running up to the murders and in what would be her, and indeed June, Nevill, Daniel and Nicholas's final hours alive. On Monday 5 August, Jean Boutell, the Bamber's housekeeper, enjoyed a coffee with Sheila and June at the farm, following which the mother and daughter went shopping in nearby Tollesbury while Jean stayed behind to look after the twins. When Jean left work at 3.30 pm that day, her final sighting of the family was of Sheila and her parents sitting in the kitchen, reading the story of *The Little Red Hen* to the boys. Sheila had been her normal self, if a little quiet. That same day Sheila and her mother also went to visit June's mother Mabel at Vaulty Farm where her housekeeper recalled that June 'looked and sounded very strained and tired'[8] during their visit. Later that evening Sheila rang another cousin, Yvonne for a chat. She says that Sheila sounded happy, and they arranged for Sheila to take the twins over to see her a couple of days later, on 7 August.

On Tuesday 6 August Jeremy was at work at the farm by 8.00 am with his father, allocating jobs to various workers with his particular task being to harvest the rape using the new tractor. Jeremy recalled seeing Sheila, June and the twins having breakfast at about 9.00 am in the kitchen and for Sheila and June, it seems they then had another busy day ahead. June was set to read the lesson at church at the 10.30

am service, and subsequently Sheila went for a wander with one of the twins down Pages Lane at around 12.30 pm where she stopped to exchange a friendly hello with Len Foakes, who recalled that 'she seemed very happy then.'[9]

By 3.00 pm that day Michael Horsnell, who was working on painting the exterior walls at Vaulty, spotted June, Sheila and the boys playing in the garden during a visit but said that it was June who was facilitating the play while Sheila was behaving, he said, 'like a Zombie.'[10] A little later, June took Sheila and the boys shopping for new jeans in a shop in Tiptree where the sales assistant said Sheila was 'vague and distant'[11] and not at all interested in her children or what they were doing. They then headed to visit an elderly friend of June's who said that they all 'seemed normal.'[12] They must have been home by 6.00 pm as a neighbour then chatted to June who was with the twins and who again seemed normal. Daniel and Nicholas were tucked up in bed by around 7.30 pm when Jeremy finally returned to the farmhouse at around 8.00–9.00 pm having finished the majority of the harvest. He found his parents and sister having supper in the kitchen but chose not to join them, instead making himself a ham sandwich and standing by the sink to eat it.

Three things which occurred that day went on to become well discussed but they, as with later events, can only be corroborated by Jeremy himself. These were a conversation he had with Sheila on the farm, an alleged argument he witnessed between his parents and sister about the twins' care, and finally his reasoning behind leaving a loaded rifle in the farmhouse before heading home for the night.

Firstly, at 4.00 pm Jeremy temporarily stopped his work on the harvest when he saw Sheila bring his nephews outside and there is some speculation that at this point, they engaged in an argument of some sort or at least had cross words as, according to some sources, Sheila's diary entry for that day contained the line 'I didn't mean to be horrible to Jeremy.'[13] Jeremy himself refutes any suggestion of an argument and claimed he doesn't remember anything of what passed between them that day, implying that it was so benign as to be forgettable.

Secondly, he recalled that during their supper, a discussion was going on between his parents and sister which he wasn't particularly involved in as he was chatting intermittently but simultaneously popping in and out. It was while he was in the kitchen, he said he saw wild rabbits outside. His later recollections about this varied and he either saw the rabbits for the first time then and rushed out immediately or had seen them previously while checking the barn and decided now would be the time to go and shoot them but no matter which is correct, he said that it happened while the others were having supper in the kitchen and discussing the twins.

Depending on whether it is thought to have any bearing on the case, what occurred that night is described by some simply as a discussion, and by some as a full-blown argument, but Jeremy claimed that it revolved around Sheila's ongoing treatment for her mental health crises, and perhaps concurrently, options for the twins' care with June and Nevill suggesting that it would be better for everyone all round if they looked into Daniel and Nicholas being fostered, with seemingly little thought as to what their father might have to say about this plan. Opinions as to whether this argument proves that Sheila was about to be tipped over the edge into a murderous rage are divided. While many believe the whole scenario was made up by Jeremy as a handy way to portray Sheila as a vulnerable ticking time bomb waiting to go off at the slightest provocation, what he said about Sheila's reaction seems at odds with this alleged motive. While he claimed that his parents told Sheila that evening that they believed the twins would be better off in foster care, he also recalled that Sheila's reaction was anything but explosive and that she 'didn't say anything, make any objections or agreements. She just appeared vacant.'[14] Was he just saying this so as not to overplay his hand? If he really wanted to plant the particular seed of Sheila reaching breaking point, why didn't he go all out and describe a full-blown argument?

Lastly, Sheila seems to have been neatly set up with a weapon with which to commit atrocities if what Jeremy said happened next is true. It was the aforementioned sighting of the rabbits in the yard which he said gave him cause to fetch his .22 Anschutz rifle in order to go outside and despatch them. A weapon of this kind is loaded via a magazine which is essentially a mechanism from which to feed ammunition into the breach of the gun ready to fire, and so it is the magazine itself which is loaded with ammunition; for this particular model the magazine had a capacity of ten rounds.

It being common sense and best practice not to openly store a loaded or even partially loaded weapon, the magazine was initially empty when Jeremy fetched it, following which he said he picked up 'a box of .22 hollow-nosed low velocity ammunition'[15] which he carried into the kitchen along with the empty magazine, having left the rifle in the scullery next to a pair of wellington boots. He tipped the box of ammunition onto the sideboard near the telephone and proceeded to load between eight and ten rounds into the magazine. He recalled that he had his back to his parents who said nothing to him during this but insisted that Sheila 'would have had a good view of what I was doing.'[16]

After loading the magazine he left the kitchen, picked up the rifle from the hallway, loaded the magazine onto the rifle, cocked it and went outside in search of the rabbits. In some descriptions of his actions, he is described as running outside, implying an urgency to get to the unwanted vermin which might then be said to account for his rather slapdash approach to gun safety which followed. He was too late, he said, as the rabbits were gone so he headed back into the scullery about five minutes later where he removed the magazine from the rifle, ejected the round that had already been loaded into the breech by his previous action of cocking the gun, and put it back in the magazine before resting the rifle up against the wall near the wellingtons. He said he left the magazine on top of an old blanket covering the settle. In another apparent rush to get somewhere or do something, he said he didn't notice if the gun and magazine were still where he had left them by the time he said goodnight to everyone at around 9.30 pm and, keen to get home, he sped out of the farmhouse, with Nevill having previously agreed to collect the last load of the harvest so that his son could get off in good time.

Later a neighbour reported hearing a shot being fired at around 10.00 pm but given that the weapon reportedly sounded like a shotgun and that Nevill was still very much alive at this time, it seems to have no bearing on the case. It's clear that Nevill was still alive as he spoke to Barbara Wilson around then and this in itself is worth recalling as she remembered the conversation leaving her feeling rather out of sorts and upset. She had not been at work that day but had called to let Nevill know that her daughter's bike was ready for them; June and Nevill had one child's bike on the farm but were after another so that Daniel and Nicholas could learn to ride them together and had agreed to take Barbara's off her hands.

Barbara recalled that Nevill was very sharp with her during the phone call, something which she described as totally out of character. He asked curtly why she hadn't come in to work that day and seemed cross with her for the oversight, despite the fact that the day off had been prearranged and agreed. As a very loyal member of staff, Barbara was very surprised at Nevill's accusatory tone and remained upset for the rest of the evening. He rather abruptly ended the phone call, and she recalled sensing impatience in his manner; she had offered to bring the bike over, but he said not to bother, and that he would pick it up the following day while delivering potatoes. 'I couldn't hear anything in the background, but something was happening at the farm that night. Mr Bamber never spoke to anyone like that – ever'[17] she said. Of course, what that something was, is still a matter for debate; following Jeremy's conviction the implication is that the tension was between father and son, while it could equally have been down to the alleged argument with Sheila about the care of her children.

June herself also took a phone call just after 10.00 pm from her sister Pamela, a courtesy call to check that Sheila and the boys had arrived safely. June told her sister that Sheila was about to go to bed but put her on the phone anyway to chat to her aunt, who recalled that it was herself who did most of the talking during the two- or three-minute-long call which she described as hard going. Sheila was much less chatty than usual, and Pamela recalled rather sadly that she didn't even say 'goodnight, Auntie Pam' as she usually would. Following this rather strained effort she spoke to her sister who confessed that she was extremely worried about Sheila and was keen for her sister's opinion on her daughter's health. Sheila had no interest in anything, even the twins, June said, and that she was trying to persuade her to take a holiday in a home in Bournemouth which, it later transpires, was actually a Christian community which perhaps validated Colin's concerns about June forcing her religious beliefs on her daughter.

One can only speculate as to what happened after Len Foakes, the last person to see the Bamber family alive, left the premises at 10.30 pm having previously seen Nevill out collecting the last load at 9.45 pm, as he had agreed with Jeremy. Various family members have attempted to shed light on the family's usual routines; Robert Boutflour said that Nevill was a strong sleeper, describing him as someone who fell asleep as soon as his head hit the pillow whereas June was a light and nervous sleeper; they habitually slept with both the bedroom window and door open. June, he said, always kept her personal Bible on her bedside table.

David Boutflour said that Nevill's usual evening routine would be to walk the dogs around the front lawn, have a shower downstairs, then relax in the lounge with a cigarette and a gin and tonic. Following this he would check the doors and windows. Reports later confirmed that the front door was bolted internally, and the back door secured with key in the mortice. The scullery door was fastened with three bolts and the dairy door was locked and bolted. The window in the dairy was slightly ajar but with a metal mesh screwed inside. David said Nevill might then settle the dogs; his wife's Shih Tzu, Crispy could be very noisy and therefore habitually slept in the kitchen. Nevill's own dog, a black Labrador named Bruce, reportedly barked whenever anyone approached the house, and therefore habitually slept in the barn. When these final routines were complete, he would head up to join his wife in bed.

By 11.30 pm, Jeremy said he was fast asleep at Bourtree Cottage, Goldhanger, approximately three miles away from White House Farm.

Oh God, I Hope She Hasn't Done Anything Silly

It is impossible for anyone other than those present at White House Farm from around 10.30 pm on 6 August 1985 to know exactly what went on between then and when Jeremy made his crucial phone call to the police at around 3.30 am. Deductions and assumptions can be made – for example we can be almost certain that Daniel and Nicholas were tucked up and fast asleep in their beds – but other than that the story can only be woven together by the evidence of those called out to the scene up until the fatal discovery of five bodies in the early hours.

The series of events which later became known to the world at large was pieced together at face value by reports from the night and indeed the days that followed, but it all started with a phone call allegedly breaking the silence in Jeremy's cottage in Goldhanger at around 3.10 am. His father, calling from White House Farm, alerted Jeremy to the fact that his sister Sheila had 'gone berserk'[1] and was in possession of a gun. Following this startling revelation the phone went dead; Jeremy said he was under the impression that someone had put their finger on the hook to terminate the call although it's difficult to tell how the distinction between a finger and a telephone receiver might be made or, at that stage, why it might be important.

Jeremy said his first thought was to try and return his father's call, but he was unable to get through because the line was engaged. Later, the distinction between a phone being off the hook and engaged would gain significance in trying to establish what happened but for now, the phone call between Jeremy and his father must have been terminated somehow, otherwise Jeremy would not have been able to do what he did next, which was to call the police.

He chose not to call the emergency services on the widely recognised 999 number, but instead to contact Witham Police Station, which is situated approximately nine miles away from Goldhanger, having searched for their number in the telephone directory. Receiving no reply from them, he followed up by trying Chelmsford Police Station, situated about fifteen miles away. Here, he got through to Police Constable Michael West and explained to him the nature of his call and the alarming activity taking place at White House Farm to which his father had alerted him.

With Jeremy on hold, West connected directly to the despatching station via radio link to inform them of the call and hence Sergeant Chris Bews and Police Constables Stephen Myall and Robin Saxby were despatched to White House Farm in car CA07 at around 3.35 am with instructions to meet Jeremy at the scene. West returned to Jeremy and advised him to head to the farmhouse where he would be met by police officers. On their journey, the officers encountered a silver Vauxhall Astra ahead of them on the Tollesbury road, later reporting that they had to pull up sharply to avoid running into the back of the car as it was driving so slowly; they subsequently overtook it and then hurried on to their destination.

It was civilian employee Malcolm Bonnett, based at the information room at Essex Police Headquarters in Chelmsford who received the call from West at around 3.26 am, although the timing of this call would later be called into question and for some, prove crucial. For now, though, Bonnett despatched car CA07 and started his radio log, the purpose of which was to record messages passed in and out of the information room. An adjacent record, the event log, was at this point started by West, its purpose being to record any messages or requests to the station from those at the scene.

Meanwhile, West had also tried calling the farmhouse himself but could not get through; he reported receiving an intermittent tone which indicated the line was engaged, or off the hook. Therefore, his next port of call was to contact British Telecom directly to request assistance in establishing the situation regarding the phones at the farm. Switchboard worker Jean Rowe subsequently checked the line and found it to be 'off the hook' at 3.42 am. She checked again at 3.56 am to find the phone still off the hook; she was able to listen in and at this point reported hearing a dog, assumed to be Crispy, barking. She heard no other noise.

The police officers who had previously been despatched in car CA07 arrived at Pages Lane off the main road leading to White House Farm at 3.48 am and at this point started and maintained the third concurrent record of events, the scene log, recording everyone who arrived during their time at the scene. A couple of minutes after their arrival, the silver Astra they had previously overtaken arrived at the scene and they were, they say, rather surprised to discover that it was driven by the originator of the earlier frantic call, and Jeremy's apparent lack of haste to get to the farm was noted by the officers present. If nothing else at this stage, they regarded it as at least unexpected and a little unusual given the circumstances and whether or not this apparent lack of urgency had a sinister undertone, Jeremy had made his very first, unfavourable impression on the Essex Police Force and it certainly wouldn't be the last time his actions elicited such a negative reaction.

Nevertheless, Jeremy confirmed to the officers that he had received a call from his father around half an hour previously and that he, Nevill Bamber, his mother, June Bamber, his sister, Sheila Caffell and her twin sons, Daniel and Nicholas, were to the best of his knowledge inside the farmhouse. Given the nature of his father's call this was an alarming set of circumstances to say the least, and in order to establish if it might be safe to attempt to enter the property, Bews asked Jeremy how many guns there might be inside and was told that there were 'lots – a few shotguns and two .22 rifles.'[2] Armed with this knowledge, Bews therefore made the decision not to make any attempt to enter White House Farm at this stage; neither himself nor any of his fellow officers were armed and as he would later explain; 'there's a standard set of rules to follow and I thought we'd either find five dead people inside the house – four murders and a suicide – or four murders and a nutter with a gun.'[3]

With Saxby staying with the car, Bews, accompanied by Myall, decided to assess the situation both visually and with help from Jeremy and they headed to the farmhouse to take a walk around. According to Myall's court testimony, from their vantage point of 'around thirty yards'[4] away it appeared that all the doors and windows were closed. Of the rooms downstairs the kitchen light was on, and the curtains open but there was no visible sign of life. Upstairs, he could see 'the centre of the house, lights on, curtains drawn closed; to the left of centre, orange curtains with a light shining behind; to the right of centre, green curtains also with the light shining behind.'[5] Jeremy confirmed for them that the 'orange' room was the bathroom, with the 'green' one being the twins' bedroom. In court, Myall confirmed that he had not noticed if the master bedroom window was open at this stage. With the kitchen exposed, they could technically have taken a look inside but Bews, no doubt with the 'four murders and a nutter with a gun' possibility at the front of his mind assessed that approaching the house unarmed would be nothing short of foolhardy. Based on this decision the group decided to walk around the perimeter of the house, prudently keeping their distance from the house. Eerily, they could hear June's dog, Crispy, barking from inside the house, and Nevill's dog, Bruce, barking from an outbuilding.

What happened next is, to those who believe Jeremy to be innocent, one of the most pivotal moments of the evening and conversely by those who believe him to be guilty, a non-event. For it was at this point that Bews said he saw what might have been movement in one of the upstairs windows. If true, this of course would confirm that while Jeremy and the police were wandering around outside, at least one member of the family was still alive inside, consequently confirming the perfect alibi for Jeremy. However, when Bews moved his position back and forth to try and replicate what he had seen, he was able to conclude that it had been a trick of the light; what he suspected to be a reflection of moonlight on the glass. Over the years Bews's recollections have changed slightly; in various interviews he's stated it was he who saw movement, or that Jeremy was the one who drew his attention to it. Nevertheless, there doesn't appear to be any contemporary reference to anyone seeing anything other than a slight movement, and certainly not a figure identifiable as Sheila, which some believe was the catalyst to what happened next, Bews radioing for armed backup.

Bews's own reasoning was that by now they had reached a kind of stalemate; Jeremy was becoming more agitated and impatient, wanting Bews to storm the building and rescue his family but Bews was not only following protocol but was becoming increasingly nervous about Jeremy's proximity to the house and already felt that his actions may well have put his civilian charge in danger. It was this he says, therefore, that precipitated the call for backup, following which he asked Jeremy to draw a floorplan of the house, partly to assist the armed police when they arrived and partly to give him something to do to keep him occupied.

While Jeremy was effectively a bystander throughout this, he did provide the officers with a good deal of background information while the wait was on. Whether it was to assist the police in establishing exactly what might be occurring inside and, perhaps more importantly, how to go about dealing with it, or whether it was to create a relentless negativity about Sheila's character, her awareness of guns, her previous psychotic episodes and serve to confirm her as the perfect scapegoat, he repeatedly made a point of referencing Sheila's mental health issues. He referenced her previous behaviours when asked if she might be dangerous by responding, 'yes, more than likely, she's tried to commit suicide several times.'[6] He confirmed that there were dangerous weapons littered about the property, which she was capable of using, explaining 'she used to come target shooting with me and she's used all the guns before.'[7]

He particularly drew their attention to the .22 rifle which he remembered having left loaded and following this realisation became reflective, hoping in what might seem with hindsight like a rather understated wish, 'Oh god, I hope she hasn't done anything silly.'[8] The group were by now back with Saxby at the car in Pages Lane and while they waited for backup to arrive, they spoke more about Sheila. It was at this stage Jeremy introduced the idea to them that when he had last seen Sheila she had been depressed, and that his parents had on the previous evening been discussing with her the potential of having the twins fostered.

Notwithstanding the fact that the language used by Jeremy to describe his sister is by today's standards considered offensive, even back in 1985 when attitudes were very different, it still apparently made the officers uncomfortable. The picture he was building of his sister was that of an unstable bomb about to explode; he called her a 'nutter', a 'depressive psychopath' and 'doolally.' However, while these descriptions might not have been the most sensitive, what he was saying was arguably not altogether untrue and indeed Bews would later use some of the same terminology when describing what he might find inside the farmhouse, indeed, a 'nutter with a gun.'

By now the group had been gathered for almost half an hour, during which Jeremy's demeanour was described as 'at times, quite jovial'[9] but before the night was out the eerie quiet would be broken by the arrival of dozens more officers of various ranks traipsing in and out of the house. For now, though, and following Bews's call for armed back up, the team, who had been out on an unarmed surveillance operation when they overheard talk of a possible firearms incident on their radios, were despatched to the farm. They had been given permission to obtain their weapons on the way by Superintendent George Harris with several units congregating at a pub in nearby Tiptree before heading collectively to Tolleshunt D'Arcy.

In advance of the armed team the first wave of backup arrived at 4.23 am in the form of cars CA05 and CA06 containing four unarmed officers. They had already been despatched as backup to CA07 before Bews's call for armed help and therefore arrived a while before the first firearms team who appeared, having collected their weapons, at around 4.58 am along with a dog unit headed up by Sergeant Douglas Adams.

Adams was shown the map created by Jeremy, assessed the scene and a plan was quickly formed. Selecting a cattle shed as the ideal vantage point from which they could view the farmhouse, he placed, amongst others, Police Constable Dermott here along with Jeremy himself, stationing several other officers around the area in order to cover the house from every angle. Dermott chatted about Sheila to Jeremy, who told him that she was a paranoid schizophrenic, but the topic of conversation changed when he was then escorted by Myall back to forward control point. He rather casually told Myall that 'if anything happened to the family, he would probably sell the caravan business and buy a Porsche' which Myall recalled thinking 'very strange, given the situation.'[10]

In the meantime, Police Constables Matthews and Macintosh were to keep a clear view of the front of the house and monitor the radio communication and Police Constable Mercer, who was equipped with body armour, was tasked with finding a containment position at the back of the house. Despite the arrival of the armed team and the formation of a plan, officers found themselves once again in a stalemate position as Police Constables Collins and Delgado continued to attempt to communicate with anyone in the farmhouse through a loud hailer. They heard no reply but for the continued barking of Crispy the dog. Adams had instructed Jean Rowe to open the phone line up again at 5.40 am and subsequently ordered it to be linked directly to the Essex Police Headquarters to allow them to continuously monitor it rather than relying on British Telecom's sporadic help. On Jean's final listen before she handed over control of the line at 6.09 am she reported that she could hear 'a very slight moving sound.'[11]

Following his instructions to Jean Rowe, for Adams the time had come to call for even more support which subsequently arrived at around 6.30 am headed up by Chief Inspector Charles Clark, Commander of the Force Support Unit. Following hot on their heels was yet another group consisting of a further ten armed officers arriving at 6.45 am, led by Inspector Ivor Montgomery. Almost immediately behind them were two ambulances which had previously been requested by Bews, with 'one for immediate use and one for standby.'[12]

Montgomery was briefed by Adams 'along the lines of four bodies and a suicide'[13] although by this point, they were still unable to tell with any certainty if anyone, specifically Sheila, was still alive inside the farmhouse. The armed officers were split into two groups with Adams to lead a group in storming the house, and Montgomery to provide containment by covering the first team on entry. They awaited the arrival of yet more officers at 7.10 am, this time headed up by Chief Inspector Terrie Gibbons, the sub-divisional commander at Witham who on his arrival assumed divisional responsibility and approved the decision for the firearms team to force entry into the farmhouse. He was followed shortly by Superintendent George Harris, the divisional commander for Chelmsford Police who had previously approved the despatch of the armed team and who was now the senior officer on scene. A plan was finally set for the first team to enter the house at 7.30 am, around three-and-a-half hours after Bews, Saxby and Myall had met with Jeremy in Pages Lane.

With trepidation, Collins and Delgado approached the kitchen, looking in through the window as they did so and checking the door, establishing that it was locked from the inside with the key still present in the lock. Collins 'caught a glimpse through the kitchen window of someone bent forward at an inexplicable angle' and radioed in that a 'female body had been sighted.'[14] Delgado noted that the telephone in the kitchen was off the hook, its receiver lying next to the cradle.

At 7.34 am the scene log records that 'five knocks on the door [were] heard over the phone'[15] in one last attempt to contact anyone living inside, following which Acting Sergeant Woodcock smashed the back door in with a sledgehammer.

Five Dead in Total

Woodcock was first into the property and found himself in the scullery, with a door to his right which, from the plans they had seen, he correctly assumed led into the kitchen, while ahead of him was another door and to the left, a set of stairs. Collins and Delgado were right behind him and headed straight into the kitchen through the door which was, if not totally closed, at least pulled to and opened inwardly from the left. Police Constables Manners and Hall were right behind them but didn't follow them into the kitchen, staying instead by the open back door to cover the scullery.

Woodcock followed Collins and Delgado into the kitchen where he was now able to see what they had already discovered, and it was truly a horrific scene. Whatever had occurred in that kitchen during the previous few hours had resulted in Nevill's lifeless body suspended awkwardly over a fallen chair next to a blood smeared AGA. His head was resting awkwardly on a coal scuttle, blood pooling around his feet and he was suffering the posthumous indignity of being found with his pyjama bottoms around his ankles. The position of his body was, according to the statements, 'behind the door and near the fire',[1] a spot which was visible from the kitchen window through which Collins had previously seen what he thought was the body of a female.

With this discovery Collins corrected his previous statement and confirmed that the body he thought was a female was evidently male, and he 'formed the opinion that he was dead.'[2] Police Constable Hall, who was armed with a shotgun and covering the scullery area along with Manners, 'heard a report from PC Collins that the body that he initially thought was a woman was in fact a man who I now know to be Neville [sic] Bamber.'[3]

One by one, the raid team entered the building and were subjected to the horrific site which had greeted Collins and Delgado. They were looking at one deceased male against the backdrop of a kitchen which was itself a mess, as though it was somehow attempting to describe to the officers what had happened to Nevill. It was clear to them that there were signs of a struggle having taken place with disarranged furniture and broken crockery in sight.

As well as the main point of entry by the back door, there were also three other doors leading from the kitchen; one diagonally opposite the back door to a hallway leading to the dining and living area and the main stairs to the master bedrooms, one adjacent to this leading to the dairy and one next to the AGA which led to the service stairs, in turn leading upstairs to a storeroom. Immediately to the left of the back door was the scullery where the team had entered, which housed a small staircase leading up to another storeroom and Nevill's office. The officers on the scene were aware, as far as they could be, of the layout of the house based on Jeremy's sketch from earlier.

By now Hall had moved into the kitchen following Police Constable Alexander-Smart's arrival to take over the cover of the scullery, where he was instructed by Collins to cover the door on the left-hand side of the room while he opened it, discovering that it led to the bottom of a flight of stairs leading to the storeroom. Hall stayed there in position covering the service stairs while Alexander-Smart allowed Acting Sergeant John Manners, Acting Sergeant Raymond Rozga and Police Constable Paul Webb access to the kitchen. At this stage, of course, they were still under the impression that there may be an assailant alive in the house brandishing a gun, and so proceeded with caution.

By now, Hall and Manners were in the kitchen with Hall guarding the service staircase, and Manners guarding the hallway leading to the dining and living area and main stairs. They were joined shortly afterwards by Webb who then guarded the entry to the dairy which Collins, Delgado and Woodcock had previously confirmed was empty.

Rozga was 'instructed by A/Ps Woodcock to maintain cover on this door [in the scullery] and stairway.' He was then 'left alone covering this door' during which he heard another member of the team in the kitchen warning 'another person not to tread in all the blood' until, after some minutes, he was 'joined by PC 172 Collins, PC 627 Delgado and A/PS Woodcock.'[4]

Collins, Delgado and Woodcock had headed back to the scullery and climbed the stairs to the office above, leaving Rozga to cover them at the foot of the stairs. While they were searching, Rozga was 'aware that PC 1437 Alexander-Smart was beside me. I could hear the officers moving about upstairs and hear the sound of someone trying to open a door which appeared to be jammed.' Woodcock then called Rozga to take their place and cover the top of the stairs while they came back downstairs to investigate further. Rozga remained upstairs in this area for 'several minutes' while trying to keep himself out of view of the team outside, and 'not wishing to distract them by seeing my movement through the windows I moved a wooden chair that was near a desk, so that I could move from their view and still keep my observations on the door.'[5]

Meanwhile, from his vantage point in the kitchen just below, Hall 'heard a noise upstairs and began to challenge up the stairs I was covering, I was calling to Sheila Bamber to make her whereabouts known to me. I was then informed that the noise I had heard was probably caused by PC Rozga who I understood was upstairs in the area of the office.'[6]

Alexander-Smart took over from Hall covering the service stairs, Collins, Delgado and Woodcock were now back in the kitchen having completed their search of the scullery and Hall now joined them, along with Webb and Manners, working their way towards the main staircase. Manners unbolted the front door at the end of the hallway 'to facilitate escape should that become necessary'[7] remembering of course, that at this point they were still keenly aware that Sheila could still be alive and armed. They had only discovered Nevill's body by this point but had now ascertained that there was nobody else on the ground floor.

By now Collins was at the base of the main stairs and, using an extending mirror to try and ascertain what was at the top, made a grim although probably not altogether unexpected discovery. He could see the reflection of the body of a deceased female. Still unsure as to what else they might find, Collins, Delgado, Woodcock, Manners and Hall climbed the main staircase. Hall covered the doors at the top of the stairs, leading to Sheila's room, a box room and the master bedroom, joined shortly afterwards by Police Constable Mildenhall who had entered the premises after the others, and who took up position covering the loft hatch.

On entering the master bedroom, they found the reflected female body to be that of June Bamber. Collins described discovering the 'body of a female person, aged about 55 years. The body was lying on the floor on her back with her head near the doorway. There were severe head injuries. I formed the opinion that she was dead.'[8]

His next discovery was two spent .22 cartridge cases, blood stains on the bed, and underneath, a small, terrified dog. It was only then that he discovered Sheila's body 'situated on the floor beside the bed on the far side of the room. The body was lying on its back. I saw what appeared to be a .22 rifle laying on top of the body with the end of the barrel near to the chin. I saw that her right hand was near the trigger of the rifle. I saw injuries to the neck and chin and what appeared to be blood had run down each side of her mouth. I formed the opinion that she was dead.' He also noted that 'next to her body I saw an open Bible.'[9]

According to their statements, Hall said that he saw 'two wounds in her throat under the chin' and Woodcock that he was 'aware that Sheila Bamber was lying flat on her back with her head slightly raised as it was against a bedside locker. She had what appeared to be two bullet holes under her chin and blood leaking from both sides of her mouth down her cheeks. The rifle was lying on the body with the muzzle close to her throat. The soles of her feet were spotlessly clean.'[10]

Along the hallway they made perhaps the most harrowing discovery of all; the bodies of six-year-old twins, Daniel and Nicholas, still lying in their beds and each having been shot in the head. It is heartbreaking how mechanically officers at a scene of this magnitude are required to describe what they found that day. One can only imagine the horror they felt on discovering the two little boys who had suffered 'severe head injuries.' Again, Collins was forced to '[form] the opinion that [they] were dead.' It was Woodstock's statement however which contains the heart-wrenching record that 'the child in the left-hand bed was lying on its right side sucking a thumb.'[11]

Jeremy, Both your Parents are Dead

Humans react in hugely diverse ways when exposed to tragic events and one cannot presume to suggest how others should process grief, tragedy or even minor, unexpected circumstances. On the face of it, Jeremy appeared distraught on being informed that his entire family were dead, this thankless task having been initially placed on the shoulders of Bews who had been with Jeremy from the very beginning of the evening.

As recalled in a later interview, Bews said that the conversation went something like this:

Bews: There's no hope for any of them. They've all been shot
Jeremy: What... everybody?
Bews: Yes. Do you want to sit down?
Jeremy: No, I'm alright.[1]

Then, Jeremy began to cry. Later, Bews recalled that he was surprised at how quickly Jeremy had broken down when he broke the news to him as, in his experience, most people initially go into shock and often don't react at all; it's not until later that the breakdown occurs. He insisted that he did not trust Jeremy right from the very beginning, evidenced by the thoughts which ran through his head as he broke the news as he recalled 'I remember thinking, that's not genuine. You're doing that because you think we're expecting you to.'[2] By some accounts Jeremy had become almost childlike following the news. When talking to Saxby he seemed confused, appearing to have trusted the officer's earlier attempts at reassuring him as he protested 'but you said it would be alright;'[3] as a child might be wounded by a parent who has lied to them, and whom they trusted would tell them the truth.

By this time more and more officers were coming and going and at 8.25 am Dr Ian Craig arrived, certifying the death of Nevill at 8.40 am, June and Sheila at 8.44 am and the twins at 8.50 am.

Even though Bews had already broken the news to Jeremy, when Chief Superintendent George Harris spoke to him a while later accompanied by Dr Craig, it provoked an unexpected and rather unnerving reaction. Jeremy asked the men where his dad was, and why he couldn't come out to talk to him; despite breaking down with Bews earlier it seemed that conversely the shock had now set in and he was unable to take in the momentous news. Feeling profoundly sorry for him in his grief, they simultaneously comforted him while trying to assert the facts.

Harris: I'm sorry, but both your parents are dead
Jeremy: I want to see him. Why can't my dad come out to see me?
Harris: Jeremy, both your parents are dead.[4]

Dr Craig proposed to give Jeremy a 'drop of whisky from a flask he had' and would later describe him at this point as 'grief stricken; and suffering 'emotional shock.'[5]

As to how the rest of the officers at the scene that night perceived Jeremy, the accounts from the lead raid team, Collins, Woodcock and Delgado all refer to Jeremy only in terms of the information he was able to relay about what was going on inside the house and they were presumably laser focused on the job in hand. It's likely they would not have given the nuances of his behaviour a second thought. He had, however had a brief conversation with Collins in attempting to find out if there was anyone in particular that Sheila might prefer to speak to if they were able to make contact, at which point he told him that 'she does like to be told she is pretty.'[6]

However, various accounts from other members of the team recall interesting snippets about their first impressions of Jeremy. Hall recorded that 'he did not strike me as being outwardly concerned about events and my initial reaction was that he was a member of the CID who was on night duty.' He does however go on to say that he 'had no conversation with this person.' When leaving the scene at around 9.00 am he said that '[Jeremy] did not strike me as being visibly distressed at this time.'[7]

Conversely, Dermott recalled that 'I returned to the vehicle in Pages Lane where I was aware of Jeremy Bamber who was sitting in an area looking in a very distressed state. I went to a nearby cottage and arranged for a cup of tea for Jeremy Bamber which as far as I know was later handed to Jeremy Bamber by the occupier of that cottage.' He had previously been alone with Jeremy in the cattle shed where they had conversed about Sheila, with Jeremy revealing that she was very depressed, a paranoid schizophrenic who had been receiving treatment and reiterated again about the alleged conversation with her parents about fostering the twins 'to which Sheila made no contribution at all.'[8]

Police Constable Jeapes also spoke to Jeremy while he was seated in the police car in Pages Lane after being told of the death of his family and recalled that he was crying, and 'appeared to be distressed', although she also went on to describe him as 'sat quietly smoking a cigarette, but I would not describe him as being distraught.'[9]

Adams recalled that Jeremy was 'visibly upset and made a request to ring his girlfriend'[10] and that on his return talked about the situation with the guns in the house, to which Jeremy replied, 'I should say the guns are locked away,'[11] indicating that we was aware that he had not followed best practice the night before and was presumably worried about getting into trouble for not doing so.

Mildenhall, Rozga, Manners and Webb all recorded in their statements that at no point did they speak to Jeremy Bamber.

Soon, two officers who would go on to play an integral part in the following investigation arrived on the scene. Firstly, at just gone 9.00 am Detective Chief Inspector Thomas 'Taff' Jones appeared along with Detective Constable Clark. They entered the master bedroom at 9.05 am and assessed the scene; according to Clark, '[DCI Jones] concluded that she had taken her own life' and there was 'no mention of calling out a pathologist, ballistics expert or biologist.'[12] Not long afterwards at around 9.15 am several more officers appeared, including Detective Sergeant Stan Jones of Witham CID and Detective Inspector Robert Miller of Braintree CID.

Taff Jones and Stan Jones could not have been more different in their policing styles, according to those who worked with them. Taff Jones was a very experienced police officer and having joined the force in 1960 he found himself working for CID just three years later. Fellow officers have since described him as 'a proud, strong-minded, hard-working individual,' and 'very dogmatic in his approach.'[13] He certainly seemed to be the type of person perhaps open to the perils of confirmation bias, described again as the sort of officer who would say 'I've made a decision' and the investigation would henceforth head in just that one direction. Jeremy's defence would later say that rather than being dogmatic in the face of perhaps opposing evidence, he simply got it right in the first place; first appearances were that Sheila had shot the family and then herself, so this is therefore likely to be exactly what happened.

Stan Jones was also very experienced, having joined up in 1961 and was described by fellow officers as very intelligent, with a 'well developed sense of humour'[14] and seemed to be more open minded than his senior ranking colleague of the same name, although Jeremy's campaign team think, some might say with good reason, that Stan Jones 'had it in for' Jeremy right from the beginning; his very first words to him were apparently 'all your family are dead, you have to be hard and strong, and the quicker you accept it the better' which was met with Jeremy calling him a 'hard bastard.' 'If I'm hard, it's for a reason', remarked Jones and by his own admission, was 'suspicious of Jeremy from the moment he set eyes on him.'[15]

According to his trial transcript, Stan Jones's first sighting of Jeremy Bamber was of him being sick or 'putting his body forwards as if he was trying to be sick'[16] when he first arrived on the scene and before entering the building. He witnessed this while talking to Dr Craig and given the time of his arrival this incident would have occurred shortly after Jeremy's odd conversation with Harris and Craig, and his consumption of the whisky which the doctor offered to him. Jeremy would later say that drinking the spirit on an empty stomach coupled with the stress of the night had caused the nausea which Stan Jones witnessed.

Perhaps because of the not altogether positive first impression he made on the officers, Jeremy continued to raise red flags both with the police and other bystanders at White House Farm that night and, indeed over the following days and weeks. Whilst still at the scene Stan Jones recalled a conversation about the family pets which he found jarring, during which he suggested that the dogs should go home with Jeremy. His suggestion, however, was met negatively with Jeremy protesting that 'I can't take them to my house, it's too small and I've got some very expensive furniture, I don't want them to ruin it. I'll have to get them put down.'[17] He eventually conceded to take his mother's dog, Crispy home with him, while leaving the Labrador Bruce in the barn for the time being. For whatever reason, Jeremy did in fact take Crispy to the vets over the next few days and have it put to sleep.

Len Foakes had by now heard the tragic news of his employers' deaths and had made his way to the farm to find out what on earth was going on. He later recalled that he was 'amazed that [Jeremy] did not seem upset in any way about what had happened'[18] especially after Jeremy had informed him that he would be expected to carry on working and even spoke of needing to get the harvest in.

Not long after his arrival Stan Jones instructed Clark to take Jeremy home. However, on hearing that Clark did not have possession of a vehicle, Jeremy offered him the use of his own car or suggested he drive them both back to Bourtree Cottage himself, which he then did. It was during the drive home that Jeremy reportedly mentioned again his plans to buy a Porsche, remarking that he 'was getting a new Porsche, a little present from the caravan site.'[19] This Porsche comment is another which comes up time and time again as alleged proof of Jeremy's materialistic and shallow attitude to life, particularly in the face of the news that his entire family had been killed. Many people simply cannot understand how it could even cross his mind to mention it in such inappropriate circumstances but again, it is for nobody to assume how people will react in such extreme circumstances. Does this comment, and indeed any of the others he made that night, come from the psyche of a cold-blooded killer, or from someone in deep shock? There is only one person who can answer that question, and that is Jeremy himself.

With the civilians gone, the police set about assessing the crime scene and by 9.30 am Stan Jones was allowed inside the building, accompanied by Miller who later remarked that 'because Taff had made up his mind, it had ceased to be a crime scene. Ordinarily, it would have been taped off for the day and only people who needed to go in there would have done. But too many boots had been in already.'[20] This attitude and action along with the following treatment of the crime scene would come back to haunt Essex Police for various reasons but not least because of various issues surrounding Sheila's body and the rifle. Not surprisingly, Sheila seems to have been the focus for the scene of crime officers and evidence from the initial statements given by the raid team all agree that Sheila was discovered with the rifle on her body, with the muzzle pointing towards her neck.

Detective Inspector Ron Cook, a Scene of Crimes Officer (SOCO), arrived to start work at the farmhouse accompanied by Detective

Constable David Bird, a police photographer. Understandably at this stage, Cook was given the impression by Taff Jones that he was looking at a suicide, which would explain although not excuse the perhaps lax and casual handling of the evidence that followed, along with his assumption that Taff Jones had been on the scene much longer than the actual fifteen minutes he had spent there and therefore that he had investigated rather more thoroughly than he had in reality. Given this assumption, it could be said that Cook and Bird took what Taff Jones told them at face value and didn't see any reason at all to question it.

Cook wasn't altogether blasé however, and did remark that 'the two wounds to Sheila's neck caused us concern'[21] given the apparent cause of her death. With hindsight this might be described as a huge understatement, given the significance these two wounds would go on to have, but for now Cook was simply following orders. He was processing the scene as a suicide and carrying out a standard examination while Bird took detailed photographs of the scene, again as instructed.

Other SOCOs on site were Police Constable Wright who had been sent from the coroner's office and Montgomery and Woodcock who had joined them inside. Cook and Montgomery proceeded to examine Sheila's body, noticing a blood stain on her nightdress, following which Cook moved her hand to facilitate Bird photographing said stain. This is the explanation, corroborated by Montgomery and Woodcock as to why there are two different crime scene photos in existence of Sheila which again, would later become fodder for Jeremy's campaign team as proof that the crime scene was somehow tampered with, or worse.

For now, though, following this photograph being taken Bird then followed his orders to remove the rifle and ensure it was safe. After establishing that the stock was damaged with pieces of wood missing and with blood on it, that the magazine was empty and that it was therefore in a 'safe, totally empty condition' he stood it against the wall in the bedroom as per his statement that 'at 11.10 the same day on request of Detective Inspector Cook, Scenes of Crime in his presence and in the presence of Inspector Montgomery I removed the gun from the body of Sheila Bamber.'[22]

They then continued to examine Sheila's body as they prepared it for removal and the officers present agreed that her nails were 'well-manicured and not broken'[23] and that she generally appeared clean, with no trace of lead dust or coating on her hands. One spent cartridge had previously been seen next to Sheila's body; when she was finally taken from the room, Woodcock confirms that he was then 'aware of two empty .22 cases which had been lying near the head and between the body and the bed on the left side of the body.'[24] By the time the SOCOs were finished they had removed a total of twenty-five cartridge cases: thirteen from the master bedroom, one from the middle landing, eight from the twins' room and three from the kitchen.

At 12.50 pm on 7 August 1985 all five bodies were removed from White House Farm and the autopsies of Nevill and Sheila were carried out on the same day. June's and those of her grandsons were carried out the following day with all the procedures being carried out by Home Office pathologist, Dr Peter Vanezis. At no point were the body temperatures of any of the victims taken, meaning that times of death could not and never have been reliably established.

Vanezis concluded that Nevill had sustained eight gunshot wounds: two to the top right of his head, two to his right temple, one to his lower lip from the left, one under the left of his chin into his mouth, one to his left shoulder, fracturing the bone and one to his left upper arm. From this he further concluded that four of the wounds to his head had been made while he was already incapacitated and that the bullets lodged in his midbrain structure would have resulted in immediate unconsciousness. Most telling of all, was that the manner of his injuries indicated that the damage to his lower lip happened in the upstairs bedroom, rendering it very unlikely, if not impossible, that he would have been able to use the telephone once he had reached the kitchen although it's not clear at this stage whether or not he realised the significance of this finding. Nevill had sustained several other injuries alongside those that killed him, including bruising to his eyes, forehead and face, lacerations to his nose, head and shoulder indicating that he had been punched or hit perhaps with a rifle stock. He also had marks consistent with pistol whipping, and three burn marks – two circular and one oval - at the base of his neck.

Sheila's autopsy revealed that her hands showed no particular sign of gunshot reside and that there was no debris on her feet or legs, although the blood-stained palm print found on her nightdress which had been photographed earlier appeared to match her right hand. She was found to have sustained two bullet wounds; the first was essentially a flesh wound with an upwards and backwards trajectory which ended in the spine but indicated that she could still have been conscious following it. However, the lack of blood drips from it would indicate that she did not stand up following this initial wound.

She sustained a further bullet wound just beneath her chin which had entered 'upwards into the hard palate of the mouth and skull and embedded in the upper part of the brain. X-rays showed the bullet as white opacity at the top of the skull with further white fragments that had broken off the bullet as it struck bone.'[25] Vanezis confirmed this wound would have severely incapacitated her and death would have occurred almost immediately following it. He ascertained that both wounds had occurred while she was lying slightly on her side and partially sitting up, and that the impact of the second bullet would have forced her down onto her back, in the position she was ultimately found.

June had been shot seven times: once above her right ear, once to the right of her neck, once to the upper right of her chest, one to the lower right of her chest, once in her right forearm, once in the outer aspect of her right knee and lastly, once between the eyes. She had sustained a bruise under her left breast which Vanezis ascertained was the result of a bullet ricochet. She also had severe bruising to her left eye which may have been the result of either a blow or the impact of a gunshot. He was unable to tell exactly the order in which the wounds occurred, but he speculated that she had started off in bed before struggling into a sitting position. She then staggered out of and round the bed and headed to the door before sustaining the fatal shot to her forehead, hitting her shoulder on the door as she fell to the floor.

Both twins were shot at extremely close range. Nicholas sustained three gunshot wounds: one on his left cheek, one to the left of his nose and one outside his right eyebrow. Daniel sustained five wounds: four in extremely close proximity near the base of skull and the last just above his left ear, forming a neat crescent.

INVESTIGATION

Long Shapely Legs

Senior investigating officer Taff Jones took the stance from his arrival at White House Farm that this tragic event was the result of a murder-suicide perpetrated by Sheila Caffell. Whether or not he made this assumption based on what he had been told by Jeremy, or from the evidence he witnessed at the scene is unknown but whatever the reason, the fact remains that the enquiry going forward at this stage was focused on Sheila as the perpetrator.

As such, by the following morning her guilt and, indeed, her intimate and personal mental health issues, were splashed all over the tabloids. The official police line and, therefore, public opinion dictated that Sheila Caffell had killed her parents and sons, and then turned the gun on herself. As a young, beautiful, vulnerable and troubled woman Sheila was perfect fodder for the press who exclaimed with relish 'Top Model Massacres Family' and 'Suicide girl kills twins and parents.'[1]

Given that this took place in 1985 when the press's treatment of those with mental health issues was less than sympathetic at best, it didn't take much at all for the general public to immediately accept that someone who was a 'nutter' or 'doolally' was capable of massacring her family and then committing suicide. Unfortunately, this can't be explained away simply because it happened 'back in the eighties' as there is no doubt that similar contemporary events still evoke such sensational headlines, with The Sun newspaper reporting in 2013 of '1,200 killed by mental patients' having previously used the descriptive phrase 'mad psycho killers.'[2] The terminology used now might be slightly more sympathetic. Not enough, but slightly.

In the initial days following the murders, it was Sheila who was on the front cover of the newspapers but Colin who seemed to be bearing the brunt of the press invasion in person. It is perhaps understandable that he was of interest to the press, but as someone who had just learned that the mother of his children has murdered them and then turned the gun on herself, it seemed needlessly ruthless and relentless to pursue him so vigorously. He described several instances of having to push his way in and out of his own home past swathes of reporters but by luck, none of the press recognised him so several of his friends were able to act as decoys over the following days to allow him to at least enter and leave his house in relatively obscurity.

The tabloids' treatment of Sheila was harsh, to say the least. Colin recalled various headlines and by-lines which in displaying the age-old misogyny we have come to expect, homed in on her looks with one describing the 'crazed killer' as a 'beautiful red head' with 'long shapely legs'[3] as if these physical attributes bore any relevance to the fact that she might have been suffering through a psychotic episode serious enough to drive her to kill her own children. Colin recalled with accuracy that 'the press ruthlessly completed Bamb's character assassination in a way that I can only describe as rape.'[4]

It should also come as no surprise that the articles played fast and loose with the actual facts of the case, with one tabloid reporting that Daniel and Nicholas, 'killed by their demented mother will be buried apart from her. Their father has refused to let them share the same resting place.'[5] The opposite was of course true; having arranged for her ashes to be buried with the boys Colin later expressed that 'it meant so much to me that her remains be placed close to the boys'[6] at their own separate funeral.

This tabloid interest was of course mainly due to the nature of the crime which had taken place but also because Sheila was a privately educated, attractive, young white female. Over the years, several studies have been made into the diverse ways in which the media portrays male and female offenders and although this is obviously a broad and emotive subject and depends on the crime and the relationship between the woman and her victim, it seems to boil down to the fact that women are generally seen by society at large as nurturing and maternal. Therefore, when they are accused or convicted of a murder, that same society feels confused, let down, and in search of a reason as to why they have become such an aberration of the traditional 'womanhood' which they have been led to expect. The reasons they therefore come up with will often be related to mental health, sex, and religion; three elements which can apparently explain away the deviancy required to kill someone, especially one's own children. It has even been suggested that women who kill are 'doubly deviant' in that they have not only broken a societal law but also one of their own gender's.

It has also become a depressing truth that some female murder victims are also treated with appalling contempt after their deaths; by use of a phrase coined fairly recently they are often referred to as the 'less dead.' This phenomenon is more pronounced in the victims of serial killers and generally refers to those who are marginalised from society or from lower socioeconomic backgrounds, examples being sex workers, migrants, and sometimes, people of colour. It's not just women at risk of this label of course, certainly homosexual men involved in sex work have also been treated as such. The phrase derives from the idea that these people are less visible; they command less positive attention in life and are, essentially, not missed by society at large, as much as, for example an upper-class white male, when they are dead.

A blatant example of this appalling treatment by the press and indeed by the investigating police force occurred during the hunt for Peter Sutcliffe, known as the Yorkshire Ripper, a serial killer who targeted and murdered thirteen women between 1975-1980. Initially, several of his victims were sex workers from the red-light district of Leeds and the surrounding areas. The police dealt with the first terrifying wave of murders by telling all sex workers simply to stay at home to keep themselves safe. The press went one step further by suggesting that really these women were partially to blame for getting themselves murdered by recklessly putting themselves in dangerous situations, as if their lifestyles were a free choice and not generally thrust on them through desperation.

Women of all socioeconomic backgrounds complained about this reaction, particularly when the police effectively set curfews on all women by telling them to stay out of public spaces after dark, resulting in said women questioning why they should be the ones forced to curtail their freedom rather than the focus being on capturing the male perpetrator. Unfortunately, this attitude is still inherently rife today; girls and women are taught not to show off too much flesh in case the boys and men surrounding them cannot control themselves, rather than looking at the problem of sexual assault and rape in a more practical way; perhaps by teaching the boys and men in question to take responsibility for their own shortcomings rather than continuing to victim blame?

It was only when Peter Sutcliffe murdered his fifth victim, fifteen-year-old Jayne Macdonald, in 1977 that the press and the police really sat up and started to take notice. Why? Because she worked in a supermarket rather than on the streets. Shockingly the police's attitude to this became all too clear and in fact immortalised during a television interview with senior investigating officer George Oldfield when he told a journalist that they were particularly worried now that the ripper was targeting 'innocent' victims. Alongside this as the, at the time unknown, perpetrator was generally believed to 'hate prostitutes' concurrent headlines stated that the ripper had made his 'first mistake' with the murder of Jayne, suggesting of course that the previous murders had been justifiable.

In terms of alleged female killers though, in Sheila's case, she also happened to be pretty, which seems to have damned her further in the eyes of the press. Not only was she a woman, because women don't do that sort of thing, but she also dared to be a beautiful woman with 'long shapely legs.' Perhaps there is an element of this which prolongs the ongoing debate about whether it was Sheila or Jeremy who was guilty of these crimes. Is it true that some people simply cannot believe that Sheila, as a woman and a mother, was capable of these crimes whereas Jeremy as a young, attractive, successful and philandering man fit the murderous bill far better than his sister?

When Sheila's name was later cleared, Colin remarked that he felt that she had been 'murdered twice', once in reality, and once in the press.

The Boss

In the meantime, some members of the investigating team were already starting to form suspicions that everything was not as it had initially seemed at the farmhouse. Not, at this stage, due to any hard evidence, but rather from the nagging thoughts that the grieving son, Jeremy, was not behaving in the way they expected him to. A few red flags had already been raised during the siege at the farm and subsequent discovery of the bodies in terms of the language he used, his perceived nonchalance and inappropriate conversations about money and cars, but it seems that Jeremy's actions over the following days started to pique an interest both in the police and his immediate family.

It is often said and remains true, that a person's behaviour and how they do or don't react during moments of extreme pressure does not prove that they are guilty of murder. However, it is also true that certain behaviours can be indicative of guilt and so while they cannot be taken as proof, they do play an important part in building a case against an individual. It is not necessarily *what* someone does, but more importantly the motivation behind their actions, which can cause concern. An example might be that of Scott Peterson who was found guilty of murdering his wife Lacey Peterson and their unborn child, Conor, in California in 2004. Most of the evidence which convicted him was circumstantial but, when put together, formed a very persuasive scenario in which he was guilty. One element was his affair with someone who knew nothing about his marriage, who in fact had been told by Peterson that he had 'lost' his wife a few months previously, before she went missing, and her body was subsequently found. His supporters say that just because he was unfaithful to his pregnant wife doesn't prove that he murdered her which is of course correct, but the motivation behind the action of telling his lover that his wife was already gone while she was still alive can prove to be nefarious and help to build up a picture of guilt.

In Jeremy's case there was more to come but it seems that his general calm and nonchalance was what first aroused suspicions. By 10.10 am on 7 August, he was back at his home in Bourtree Cottage with Clark where he made himself a bacon sandwich before telling the officer that he was ready to make his statement about the events of the previous night. This seemingly innocuous act is described by Jeremy as a quick bite to eat but later by some as a full fry up. It has therefore become perhaps rather more significant than the action itself warranted, due to the casual manner in which it was carried out.

One viewpoint is that grief should have made it impossible for Jeremy to even think about food, having just learned that his entire family had been massacred. On the other hand, Jeremy's explanation was that he had earlier drunk some whisky on an empty stomach which had made him sick. This, coupled with the obvious stress he had been under for the previous few hours had made him feel nauseous and that he just needed some food to settle his stomach. 'I microwaved two slices of bacon to have in two slices of toast, that's all I had in the fridge to eat quickly' he says, dismissing those who say 'Bamber's definitely guilty cos he ate a bacon sandwich and drank coffee' as 'absurd.'[1] Nevertheless, it reportedly struck Clark as 'odd' at the time.

As he settled down to take Jeremy's statement, a trickle of people began arriving at Bourtree Cottage. First was his cousin, Ann, followed by Stan Jones and then Jeremy's girlfriend Julie. Ann's brother David arrived later, as did her husband Peter and at around lunchtime, Robert and Pamela, Ann and David's parents, arrived under their own steam. David would later say that he was alerted due to the news that there was a police helicopter on the scene and had headed initially to the farm where he was refused access, following which they had rushed to Jeremy in support. Colin and his girlfriend Heather also arrived shortly afterwards, having been transported by police car from London, where he had had the horrific news broken to him on the doorstep of his flat.

And so it was that Jeremy found himself surrounded by, arguably, the surviving family members who knew him and Sheila the best, or at least those who had known them both since childhood and understood the Bamber family dynamics and Sheila's mental health struggles. The more they witnessed of what Jeremy said and did over the next few hours, days and indeed weeks, and the more they tried to imagine Sheila as a multiple murderer, the more it worried them.

First and foremost, Clark was tasked with taking Jeremy's statement and right off the bat Ann reportedly started to become suspicious of her cousin. She had already begun to take notes of everything Jeremy said, as if aware that it might be significant at a later date and picked up on a couple of things in particular; she found Jeremy's account of the conversation between her aunt, uncle and Sheila the previous night difficult to swallow, finding it impossible to imagine them being so heartless as to suggest putting the children into foster care. Jeremy's description of his relationship with his father being like that of a normal son also rankled with her, being aware of a tension which had existed between them. Colin was also called upon to make a statement about his ex-wife, which was recorded by Stan Jones, and he recalled Jeremy asking him afterwards how many pages he had got through in his statement, rather gleefully reporting that he had 'done over twenty-four' pages in comparison to Colin's eight, a bragging and oddly competitive attitude to the task at hand which he thought was 'strange.'[2]

Stan Jones said that he witnessed an exchange between Julie and Jeremy during his visit to the cottage which at the time simply caught his attention as being unusual; he heard what he described as a sort of a chuckle behind an almost-closed door and on entering the room saw the couple quickly pull apart as if they had been in an embrace of some sort and looked rather sheepish at being caught. Julie later put forward an extremely damning, for Jeremy, explanation as to the nature of their conversation in that room but again, for now, it was added to the mental list of minor incidents which had caught the attention of the police and family.

Some of the allegedly suspicious behaviour such as this was witnessed first-hand, but some has developed a myth-like quality over time, some might say without any real basis. One such example might be that during Stan Jones's brief stay at the cottage, he asked Jeremy if he would like any heavily bloodstained items from the farmhouse destroyed. Jeremy agreed, asking for anything valuable to be salvaged. Over the years this seems to have taken on perhaps more significance than it deserves, implying that immediately following the murders Jeremy asked for everything in the house, and therefore any potential evidence which might be contained within it, to be destroyed. It followed that several pieces of bloodied evidence *were* burnt shortly after the house had been cleared, for example the mattresses and bed sheets.

Would these items have been useful, if not vital, had the police been carrying out a murder enquiry rather than assuming that the deaths were a result of a murder-suicide? Quite probably. If Jeremy requested that the items be burned immediately, could that come across as suspicious? Again, yes. However, the evidence suggests that this course of action was *put to him* rather than requested *by* him and doesn't seem to have raised any red flags at the time. If anything, this rush to clear the house and burn the evidence shines a negative light on the police rather than Jeremy, as they were keen to close the case, with no intention of embarking on a thorough investigation into the events of 7 August. One can't deny, however, that no matter who instigated the disposal of the material it did Jeremy's defence a huge favour; while it's likely that it would have corroborated the series of events which were later proven in court, it can never be stated with one hundred per cent certainty that it might not also have proved Jeremy's story; frustratingly, we can never be sure.

Nonetheless, following the afternoon spent at Bourtree Cottage Ann, Peter and Robert spent the evening at home together, discussing the events of the past twenty-four hours. For them, even at this early stage, it wasn't just the niggling doubts about Jeremy that were creeping in but almost more importantly, they were really struggling to imagine Sheila being capable of the murders. For them, the hypothesis that Sheila shot her parents, children and then herself just did not add up; for a start none of them was convinced that Sheila could use a gun at all, never mind kill her entire family with near pinpoint accuracy with one but at this stage, they had no hard evidence to the contrary.

While Sheila's motives had been accepted immediately by the public, this conviction was certainly not shared by the family and more importantly given that she was accused of killing his beloved children, nor by Colin who was simultaneously experiencing the same doubts. By his own account, at first, he grudgingly accepted the official police line while overcome with heart-breaking grief over the loss of his sons but even then, he didn't blame Sheila and struggled to imagine her acting in such a way. Her suicide was probably the most believable element to him, and he could just about conceive that she may have been violent towards her mother, given their tumultuous relationship but not to her father and absolutely, certainly, not towards her sons whom she adored.

Initially, Colin had assumed that a shotgun had been used in the killings; although still unlikely, he could just about see Sheila picking one up and shooting it in a rage but the murder weapon, having been found on Sheila's prone body, had now been ascertained as the semi-automatic .22 Anschutz rifle. When he learned what the family had been killed with, he realised that this rendered the idea of her killing anyone even more unlikely, if not impossible. Years later, he would say that 'Bambs wouldn't have had the first idea how to use [a semi-automatic rifle], let alone reload it.'[3]

As they soon discovered from the post-mortems, a total of twenty-five shots were fired on the night of the murders, each one hitting its target with relative and sometimes pinpoint accuracy. The magazine on a .22 Anschutz rifle can only hold a maximum of ten rounds of ammunition at one time, meaning that the magazine would have to have been reloaded at least three times throughout the killing spree and the thought of Sheila being able to reload this rifle and shoot it twenty-five times on target was enough to raise serious doubts in Colin and the family. The police, however, were still under the impression that Sheila was familiar with guns based on what they were told by Jeremy, and at this stage Jeremy alone.

Not only that, but the family found the whole business of Jeremy leaving a loaded gun lying around in the scullery, and Nevill then not ensuring that it was made safe and stored away just unbelievable, given how fastidious Nevill was and always had been about gun safety. They also discussed other concerns; Ann couldn't imagine why on earth Nevill would call Jeremy under such circumstances rather than calling for the emergency services, or indeed why he would bother making a phone call at all rather than simply having it out with his much smaller and physically weaker daughter. The phone calls in general particularly bothered her; for example, why didn't Jeremy call 999? It had also since come out that he had telephoned Julie at around the same time as he called the police that morning; why had he done that? Jeremy's explanation that he didn't think it was important enough to warrant a 999 call baffled her and by the end of an exhausting evening they had, between them, if not concluded then at least speculated that it was more likely that Jeremy had killed his parents than Sheila.

The following day on 8 August Jeremy met with the family solicitor Basil Cock who, in contrast to some others apparently found Jeremy's behaviour 'in keeping with his bereavement',[4] and it was following this meeting that the family learned that Jeremy had decided to have his parents cremated despite their wishes expressed in life to be buried. His reasoning, he told them, was because 'they were not whole'[5] and whether or not this particular piece of unwelcome news was the catalyst, Ann and Anthony decided that day that they would take their concerns to the police. As such they, accompanied by David, arranged to meet both Taff Jones and Stan Jones the following day.

It did not go well. Although Stan Jones was pleasant, Taff Jones took umbrage with what he perceived as their interference, reportedly referring to Ann as 'Miss Marple' and shouting at her to 'stop writing'[6] in reference to her prolific note taking throughout the meeting which he clearly found off-putting and possibly took as a criticism of his own efficacy. The family's concerns about Sheila's ability to have carried out the murders were dismissed and they headed home, discouraged.

Despite being in deep shock and grieving for their lost loved ones and, evidently suffering with the added complication of suspecting their cousin of being involved, the family still needed to attend to the practicalities involved following a death. Therefore, in the days following the murders they started to put various security measures in place and following their meeting with the police, Ann, Anthony and David headed to a meeting to discuss the future of the farm with Jeremy, Peter and Chris Nevill, another cousin. It was during this meeting that Jeremy reportedly announced that he was planning to instruct Sotheby's to value the contents of the farm and then store them prior to selling them all on.

While not documented fully, Ann implies ambiguously that she, Anthony and David then accused Jeremy of the murders during this meeting or at the very least put their reservations and suspicions to him. Jeremy was reportedly so anguished by the accusation that it resulted in him being prescribed Valium to calm him down, so one can only imagine the atmosphere hovering over them that day. To exacerbate it further, it was during this meeting that Ann made the rather callous remark that for the funeral, they should only order black flowers for Sheila's coffin. Ann would later say that she said this purely in an effort to antagonise Jeremy into some sort of reaction although she apparently failed when Jeremy allegedly did not reply to this apparent snub but was, he says, deeply hurt by it. It also had a deep impact on Colin when he heard about it who, although not a specific target for Ann's hurtful sentiment was nonetheless distraught if not unsurprised at this thoughtless comment given that he had never really been accepted by Sheila's family.

Unbelievably, the atmosphere must have calmed down to a certain extent as later that day, Jeremy headed to yet another a meeting at which Ann's husband Peter accepted his offer to manage White House Farm and Ann agreed to find a security team to watch over it while Jeremy and Julie visited Colin in a pre-arranged trip to stay with him in London. At this stage Jeremy hadn't been back to the farm and made it clear that he had no intention of doing so, following which Ann also agreed to be the key holder for the farm and the new security system when it was installed. This of course gave her and the family unrestricted access, with Jeremy's knowledge and blessing, to White House Farm.

It was following Jeremy and Julie's return a couple of days later on 12 August that things seemed to come to a head within the family yet again, this time with the focus of the conflict being the possessions at White House Farm. Despite his earlier assertion that he did not want to return to his family home, during a pre-arranged meeting with Peter to discuss his management of the farm, Jeremy and Julie agreed to meet him there, along with David and Ann, during which she showed Jeremy the new alarm system and handed him his new key.

While Ann and David were already concerned with what they thought of as Jeremy's inappropriate behaviour they were, they say, more specifically horrified on this day at his greedy and impatient attitude towards his potentially huge inheritance as evidenced by his swift plans to sell everything off. Some say however that it was the family themselves who were desperate to sort out the financial arrangements and get their hands on their fair share of Aunty June and Uncle Nevill's estate and subsequently nobody comes out of the meeting on 12 August in a particularly good light. The behaviours displayed by everyone involved could at best be described as strange, even given the circumstances leading up to them.

Firstly, Ann offered to show Jeremy around the farmhouse to explain where each of the bodies had been discovered, perhaps studying his reactions for some sign of involvement. At best her actions might be described as insensitive and at worst reckless, given that she had decided by this time that he was guilty of the murders, although one imagines that she seemed fairly secure in the knowledge that Jeremy would be unlikely to try and retaliate violently in broad daylight. In fact, he did the opposite, as according to them he was petrified during the tour, unwilling to enter certain rooms and physically shrinking away at times. This could be construed in two ways; that his horror was caused by imagining the fates that befell his family or, as the family perceived it at the time, that he was reliving exactly what had happened, having been there when it did.

What happened next is often held up by Jeremy's supporters as proof that the wider family were money grabbing vultures intent on making sure Jeremy didn't get a single penny of what they perceived as their rightful inheritance. Or was it that their actions were born out of sheer panic that this man had, as they suspected, killed his parents and was about to get away with not only that but also as a consequence, with a huge fortune which they felt duty bound to protect on behalf of June and Nevill?

Either way, Jeremy's attitude changed when they arrived back at the kitchen, where, on checking the various rooms, Jeremy discovered that his father's wallet full of cash was missing and reported it stolen while it had, in fact, been Ann who had taken the cash along with various other possessions when she had visited a couple of days previously. She, David and Robert had begun to clear the house that day and had removed jewellery belonging to June, amongst other valuable items. It was during this visit that they had also found something which would go on to be pivotal in the case against Jeremy but which, for now, perhaps prudently, they did not mention.

Jeremy was reportedly livid that his relatives had taken his parents' belongings from the house, arguing that he had only agreed for them to keep the house safe, not strip it of its assets. In contrast, the family say that they were just trying to make sure that he didn't get his hands on absolutely everything, a worry which they argued was well-founded and vindicated a couple of days later when Ann discovered Jeremy at White House Farm accompanied by Basil Cock and the team from Sotheby's going through the house and documenting its contents ready for sale, just one week after its occupants had been murdered. While these events could arguably be explained away by family rivalry, greed and the result of grief, no matter what the motivation behind them, the speed with which everyone involved seemed to scrabble for engagement rings, priceless portraits and cold hard cash seems disrespectful at best.

However, the worst, or perhaps the most damning, behaviour so far was about to rear its head with the largest red flag of all appearing at the funerals of Nevill, June and Sheila on 16 August 1985.

Given the huge public interest in the case, St Nicholas's church at Tolleshunt D'Arcy was inevitably surrounded by press and television crews on the day. What was subsequently broadcast on the news portrayed an apparently grief-stricken young man in the unenviable position of burying and mourning his parents and sister who had been wrenched from him in the cruellest way imaginable. Viewers also saw his loving girlfriend supporting him both emotionally and physically as he, at times, seemed to falter and break down under the stress as he left the church following the service, with his anguished former brother-in-law just steps behind him.

What the family and to a certain extent, the police, saw behind the scenes was very different. Of course, they witnessed the display of grief along with the rest of the nation, but what the public weren't privy to were the preparations at Bourtree Cottage before the event, and the wake that was held there afterwards during which Jeremy's behaviour reportedly made several of the attendant guests feel uncomfortable at best. It began with Jeremy's rather perky remark that 'I hope they get my good side!'[7] as he set the video in anticipation of capturing the news coverage later that day.

Following the funeral itself, David recalled that Jeremy's apparent grief in front of the cameras which had rendered him almost unable to walk, had disappeared as soon as he was out of the public gaze. Jeremy relaxed immediately, he said, displaying a large 'chilling' grin on face. It was on seeing this that David recalled his brother-in-law Peter turned to him and said, 'he did it, didn't he?' to which David regrettably agreed, reflecting 'that's the point where we hadn't got any doubts.'[8]

Jeremy himself seemed oblivious to the reactions he was causing. On the journey to the crematorium, he had reportedly cracked 'smutty jokes' and back at Bourtree Cottage at the wake was in positively high spirits, showing off his Hugo Boss suit, pointing to the label and telling onlookers 'that's me now – the Boss.'[9] Detective Inspector Miller represented Essex Police at the funeral and the wake and was shocked at this lack of respect shown by the recently bereaved man.

It wasn't just the 'boss' comment which had elicited this emotional reaction; back at the church Miller had remarked to his colleague, Detective Constable Barlow that he believed Jeremy's grief to be an act, and it appears he wasn't the only one watching who drew the same conclusion. Jeremy's former housemaster, William Thomas, felt so strongly that his former pupil's outburst on screen was insincere that he contacted Miller to warn him. Detective Chief Inspector Mike Ainsley, who would eventually head up the following murder investigation, was watching the funeral at home with his wife, who immediately pointed to Jeremy following his appearance on camera and declared, 'he did it'![10]

Despite the negative reactions his behaviour elicited, these feelings were not shared by everyone. Later that evening following the funeral Jeremy, Julie, Liz, Brett Collins, who had recently flown in to support Jeremy and Julie's friends Karen and Andy Bishop decided to go out to eat at a local restaurant, the Caribbean Cottage which they frequented regularly and where they were well-known by the owner, Rodney Brown, and where they purportedly 'ate well and drank heavily.'[11]

Of this, Julie said Jeremy was in high spirits, laughing and joking throughout the evening. Conversely Rodney Brown, also a friend of Jeremy's spoke up at the time and has since been interviewed for a documentary and gave quite the opposite account. His recollection is that while the group were indeed ordering food and drinks, this was simply by way of his friends trying to cheer him up and make him laugh; he admitted they were drinking heavily but, he said, this was to 'wash away the memories of the day.'[12] Of the funeral, Jeremy himself said that 'I'm sure that I wasn't being completely rational in the way that I was trying to handle the loss of my family, and I know that with friends, that I was paying for a few more meals and drinking a bit more and things like that because I wanted to feel loved.'[13]

Inheritance

There are no two ways of looking at it; following the death of his parents Jeremy was likely to inherit a substantial amount, particularly given that Sheila and the twins were no longer alive to benefit from their share. Nevill and June's wills had not at this point been read but it was safe to assume that Jeremy, along with David and Ann, would at least be looking at a share of June's estate which included her forty-two per cent share of the Osea Road caravan park, of which Jeremy and Ann already shared the remaining sixteen per cent.

By the time of his death Nevill had increased his already substantial property portfolio; as well as inheriting his mother's property, Clifton House, he now also owned Bourtree Cottage where Jeremy lived and the Maida Vale Flat he and June had purchased for Sheila. Nevill had given a twenty-five per cent share of Clifton House each to his niece and nephew, Jacqueline and Anthony, leaving him with fifty per cent to pass down to Jeremy. There seemed to be a fair amount of money tied up in Clifton House alone; Nevill had reportedly lent Jacqueline and Anthony money for their share of the planned renovation to turn the house into five separate flats, with the idea that their subsequent sale would be more than sufficient to cover the full renovation costs.

Nevill and June's joint business interest N&J Bamber Ltd at that time managed around 750 acres of land and counted amongst its assets several valuable items of farm machinery, and included Little Renters Farm which Nevill purchased in November 1984 on behalf of Peter and Ann. When the wills were eventually read in early January 1986, June's estate was valued at £230,000 and Nevill's at £380,000 and N&J Bamber Ltd was estimated to be worth £400,000. By today's standards, at the time of writing, this represents a total of more than £3 million. Even before the official reading, Jeremy and his family would have been aware of the approximate value of June and Nevill's combined estates and clearly, if convicted of murder, Jeremy would never see a penny and the estate would then naturally pass to other members of the family.

And while the inheritance itself appears to be a very strong motive for Jeremy to have killed his entire family it also appears to be the crux of one of the arguments put forward by Jeremy's supporters. While they are not claiming that Ann, David and family were literally responsible for the deaths of Nevill, June, Sheila, Daniel and Nicholas, they do claim that they unfairly and relentlessly pointed the finger at Jeremy, steering the police away from believing that Sheila was responsible and that they did this for one reason only; so that he would not inherit what they felt was rightfully theirs. What better way to ensure they ended up with absolutely everything than to ensure that Jeremy was incarcerated for murder?

This accusation is not a frivolous one put forward only by loyal supporters; it was later referenced at the trial, with the jury giving some not inconsiderable thought to the idea that the family might have an ulterior motive in seeing Jeremy convicted and therefore whether or not their evidence was to be trusted. There is no denying that, no matter what the motives, nobody in the family comes out of this in a particularly favourable light and notwithstanding any accusations, the division of assets was certainly not rectified in a particularly dignified manner.

After the altercation at White House Farm on 12 August, David and Ann explained they were so concerned about Jeremy getting his hands on what they perceived as their share of the estate that they took what could be described as rather underhand, albeit understandable, action. June's mother, Mabel Speakman, was by this time 95 years old and, for reasons best known to them, her family had not yet told her about the murders at White House Farm and she had been told that the family were simply on holiday. Mabel's housekeeper was horrified that the news was being kept from her and threatened to leave her employment unless she was told. As a result, twenty-two days after the murders, on 29 August, Pamela broke the news to her mother that June, Nevill, Sheila and the twins were dead. She reportedly did not mention Jeremy, and Mabel did not ask after him.

Following this revelation, Mabel decided that she wanted to change her will, leaving everything she owned to her remaining daughter, Pamela. Her original will had been split fifty-fifty between her two daughters and as such, Jeremy held a claim on June's half. With this change in the will, he would receive nothing. Robert facilitated everything, calling in a solicitor at his mother's request and becoming co-executor, alongside a member of the firm. Robert maintained that Mabel was not only of sound mind but was keen if not impatient to confirm the changes, even commenting to him that she wanted to hurry up and sort it out 'before I die.'[1]

Jeremy's supporters maintain that Mabel was coerced into making the changes and what is unclear here is exactly what, if anything, she knew about Jeremy's alleged involvement at this stage. The family allude to the fact that they simply didn't mention him. Jeremy claimed that he was prevented from visiting his grandmother and that he believes she was coerced into changing the will with his campaign team going one step further with the allegation that the family had told Mabel that Jeremy was also dead, thus negating any need for him to feature in the will at all.

The Boutflours concede that their motive behind facilitating the change was to stop Jeremy getting his hands on this half of the Speakman estate as they understood he was planning to sell it as soon as he could. They also conceded that this may put them under an element of suspicion given that they now had a motive to inherit a larger share of June's bequests, even more so because the land Jeremy was intending to sell included the aforementioned Little Renters Farm. So, it seems fairly clear and undisputed that the family arranged this change in Mabel's will in order to stop Jeremy from inheriting, but was this down to malice or simply a justifiable desire to keep what was rightfully theirs from being sold?

No matter which, it wasn't just the family who took issue with Jeremy's mercenary attitude towards the family heirlooms. Again, the often-forgotten Colin, who certainly had no financial motive for wanting Jeremy convicted and no stake at all in the contents of White House Farm or indeed the property itself, recalled a very hurtful episode which took place at Sheila's flat in Maida Vale a month after the murders. By now Jeremy seemed to have unofficially moved into the flat along with Brett Collins, and Colin had arranged a visit to take on the unenviable and harrowing task of going through, sorting and removing his sons' belongings.

On arrival, Colin found evidence that Jeremy had moved quite a few of the valuable items from White House Farm to the flat, presumably to facilitate selling them at auction houses in London. A much-admired portrait of 'Granny Bamber' was sitting at the foot of the stairs, ready for a Sotheby's valuation. Colin was horrified that Jeremy was planning to sell such a precious family heirloom, but Jeremy confirmed that he had already managed to sell 'virtually everything'[2] from the stash he had brought from the farm to an antique dealer who 'bought all of it for cash.' He did however quantify this by saying that he needed the money to 'pay for the massive death duties'[3] which would come from his inheritance.

Colin was distraught, not least because he had been planning to ask for some of the more sentimental items to keep for himself, even if it meant buying them, but they were now practically all gone. Much worse was in store for him though, as his trip to painstakingly go through Daniel and Nicholas's belongings had been utterly wasted when he discovered that Jeremy and Brett had already cleared the

Family photo of (L-R) June Bamber, Sheila Caffell, Jeremy Bamber, Colin Caffell and Nevill Bamber. Date Unknown. SWpix.com/APA

Nevill and June Bamber at White House Farm with their dogs, Labrador Bruce and Shi Tzu Crispy. Date Unknown. SWpix.com/APA

Family photo of Sheila Caffell and her sons Daniel Caffell (L) and Nicholas Caffell (R). Date Unknown. SWpix.com/APA

June Bamber with her adopted daughter Sheila Caffell and grandsons Daniel and Nicholas Caffell. Date unknown. Mirrorpix / Alamy Stock Photo

Bourtree Cottage, Goldhanger. Jeremy Bamber's home at the time of the murders. 27 July 2024.

White House Farm, Tolleshunt D'Arcy Essex. The Bamber family home and scene of the horrific events which took place on 7 August 1985. 17 October 1986. Mirrorpix / Alamy Stock Photo.

View through the window into the kitchen at White House Farm where Nevill Bamber's body was discovered. August 1985. SWpix.com/APA

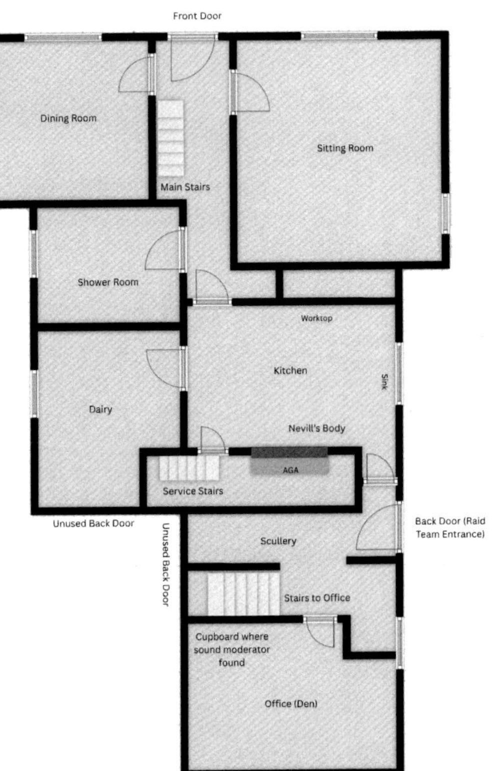

Plan to show the ground floor of White House Farm at the time of the murders. Not to Scale.

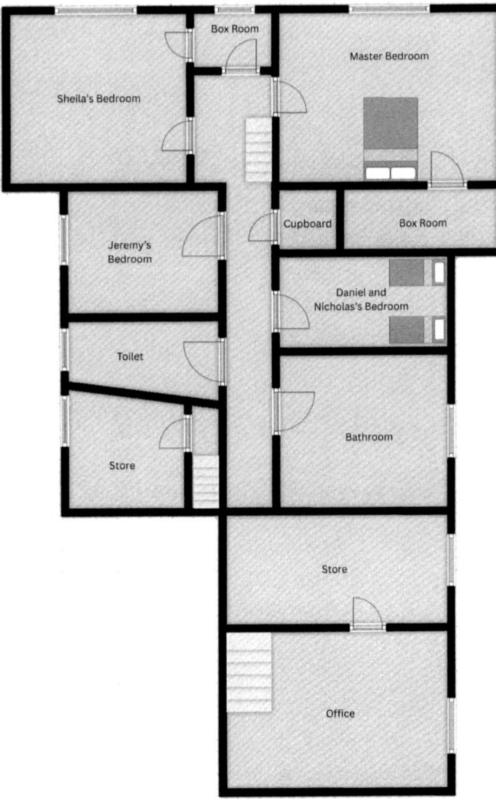

Plan to show the first floor of White House Farm at the time of the murders. Not to Scale.

Exhibits Officer PC Chris Whiddon during a press conference at Essex Police Headquarters, holding the murder weapon, the .22 Rifle and silencer. 28 October 1986 PA Images/Alamy Stock Photo

Julie Mugford arriving to give evidence at Chelmsford Crown Court in the trial of Jeremy Bamber. 8 October 1986 PA Images/Alamy Stock Photo

Julie Mugford supporting Jeremy Bamber at the funeral of his parents and sister, accompanied by Colin Caffell. 16 August 1985 Mirrorpix/Alamy Stock Photo

Jeremy Bamber being led into Chelmsford Crown Court at the start of his trial. 6th October 1986 Mirrorpix/Alamy Stock Photo

David Boutflour, Jeremy's cousin, arriving at Chelmsford Crown Court. 7 October 1986. PA Images/Alamy Stock Photo

Anne Eaton, Jeremy's cousin, arriving at Chelmsford Crown Court. 7 October 1986. PA Images/Alamy Stock Photo

Colin Caffell, Sheila's ex-husband, accompanied by Robert Boutflour, Jeremy's uncle, as they attend his trial. 7 October 1986. PA Images / Alamy Stock Photo

Detective Sergeant Stan Jones (L) with Acting Chief Superintendent Mike Ainsley (C), outside the court during Jeremy Bamber's trial. 4 October 1986. Mirrorpix.

Jeremy Bamber leaving Chelmsford Crown Court after being found guilty of the murder of his adoptive parents, his sister Sheila and her six-year-old twins at White House Farm. He had been told that he must serve a minimum twenty-five years of a life sentence. 28 October 1986. Mirrorpix/Alamy Stock Photo

Jeremy Bamber, jailed for life in 1986 for the murders of five members of his family at White House Farm in Essex, arriving at the Court of Appeal in London. 17 October 2002. PA Images/Alamy Stock Photo

Julie Smerchanski, formerly Mugford, as she leaves the Court of Appeal in London. 24 October 2002. PA Images/Alamy Stock Photo

(L-R) Philip Walker (JBIC), Peter Tatchell, human rights campaigner and Yvonne Hartley (JBIC) hold a protest alongside other supporters outside the headquarters of Essex Police, demanding the release of evidence which they say will prove Jeremy's innocence. 25 November 2021. JBIC Ltd

DEAR HELEN,
THANK YOU FOR YOUR LETTER,
THERE IS NOTHING IN THE RULES
THAT PREVENTS ME TALKING
ABOUT MY CASE – I DO, AND,
BORE PEOPLE TO TEARS NO
END OF TIMES IM SURE.
I KNOW ALL ABOUT THE
VARIOUS DISCUSSION GROUPS,
SOME I ENGAGE WITH, LOTS
OF THEM ARE FULL OF TROLLS
AND STRANGE MIXTURES
OF PEOPLE DISCUSSING CASE
STUFF THAT COMES FROM A
BOOK, OR DRAMA PROGRAMMES
THAT IS FOR THE MOST PART
JUST MADE UP NONSENSE.
ITS NOT ALL MADE UP I
KNOW THAT – BUT THE TRUTH
CAN GET SO TWISTED OUT
OF SHAPE WHEN THERE IS
NO ONE TO STRAIGHTEN
THINGS OUT WITH QUOTES
AND STUFF FROM OFFICIAL
DOCUMENTS.
AND THAT PHRASE "ONLY

Letter from Jeremy Bamber to the author. February 2021.

2

YOU KNOW WHAT REALLY HAPPENED" I HAVE NO MORE CLUE THAN ANYONE ELSE WHO STUDIES THE CASE MATERIAL – I DO HAVE MULTIPLE ALIBIS COS SHEILA WAS ALIVE IN THE HOUSE FOR HOURS AFTER ME AND AROUND 50 ODD COPS AND PARAMEDICS HAD ARRIVED AT THE SCENE. WHAT HAPPENED INSIDE THE HOUSE CAN ONLY BE PUT TOGETHER FROM ALL THE DIFFERENT TESTIMONY FROM ALL THE VARIOUS WITNESSES WHO SAW SHEILA MOVING AROUND IN THE HOUSE, SAW LIGHTS GOING ON AND OFF AND CURTAINS BEING OPEN-ED AND CLOSED, SOME COPS TALKED TO SHEILA, SHE MADE A 999 CALL AT 6:09 AM WHICH IS WELL DOCUMENTED IT'S AGREED I WAS WITH VARIOUS POLICE OFFICERS FROM 03:50 AM TILL WE LEFT WHITE HOUSE FARM MID MORNING SO I'VE NO MORE INSIGHT THAN ANYONE ELSE.

Letter from Jeremy Bamber to the author. February 2021.

St Nicholas's Church, Tolleshunt D'Arcy. June and Nevill Bamber were actively involved in the church community and are now buried in the grounds. 27 July 2024.

Plaque at St Nicholas's Church, Tolleshunt D'Arcy commemorating June and Nevill Bamber. 27 July 2024.

twins' room in its entirety to make way for Brett to use, dumping the contents in black bin bags. This utter betrayal, Colin said, left him feeling 'heartbroken and violated.'[4]

As if things couldn't get any worse, Jeremy then showed Colin that he had discovered a number of albums containing photographs of his sister Sheila, gleefully pointing out several nude ones, of whose existence Colin had been totally unaware. This in itself while perhaps distasteful was not so much the worrying thing, but that his former brother-in-law's manner was 'more like that of an immature schoolboy ogling his first girly magazine' rather than a man 'looking at photographs of his dead sister.'[5] It is alleged that Jeremy went on to attempt to sell if not these photographs, then other nude images of his sister to The Sun newspaper.

Discoveries

So far, so much speculation. While these events did not build a particularly positive image of Jeremy, or of his family, they did not prove anything at this stage apart from perhaps establishing a possible motive for Jeremy to have carried out the murders. There was no solid proof.

While the police were unwilling to change their minds based on the family's gut feeling about Sheila being unable to carry out the murders, things did however start to move in a different direction when more potentially hard evidence to throw doubt on the scenario of a murder-suicide began to emerge. The police, of course had initially treated the crime scene with that very scenario in mind and therefore, once the bodies had been cleared, the house was essentially left for Jeremy and his wider family to do with what they pleased and it was because of this free-range access that just three days after the murders, on 10 August, during a visit to White House Farm the family made the most vital and perhaps contentious discovery of all. It would begin to implicate Jeremy in the murders but ironically, the very nature of how it was discovered left a question mark, for some, over its evidential value forever.

Ann arrived on her own early that morning and set about cleaning and sorting the house now that the police had finished with it. David arrived at around 11.00 am followed later in the afternoon by their father, Robert, accompanied by Basil Cock, June and Nevill's solicitor. The meeting at the farm had, Basil said, been arranged at Ann's instigation as she was planning on finding and then relocating any valuable items for safekeeping with Basil. Later Barbara Wilson was called out to help with some legal questions following the opening of the farm's safe which contained Nevill and June's wills. Bearing in mind this visit took place the day after their alleged confrontation with Jeremy about his part in the murders and who was now in London with Julie, it seems this timing was not just coincidental.

Apart from a few minor discrepancies, those present at the time essentially all agreed with the witness statement David made on 17 September 1985 about the activity in the farmhouse that day leading up to and following the discovery. David was searching the under stairs cupboard which contained a variety of items including guns and ammunition but most striking of all was a 'Parker & Hale type gun silencer about seven inches in length and about one inch in diameter, standing upright'[1] on the shelf. Striking, perhaps, as he recognised it as being the silencer, or sound moderator, belonging to the .22 Anschutz rifle known to be the murder weapon.

At this point, this discovery may well not have raised any alarm bells at all, but it certainly piqued his interest enough to remove it from the cupboard, following which he carried it into the kitchen to show his sister and father. Upon further examination they spotted 'deposits of what appeared to be red paint' and 'a spot the size of a match head, coloured red on the leading face of that knurled end' as well as a 'fresh silver coloured scratch mark about one inch long about halfway along its length.'[2] Again, nothing to necessarily raise alarm bells but perhaps intriguing nonetheless, certainly enough for David to load it into Ann's car along with various other items they were in the process of retrieving, such as June's jewellery. He then headed back to Oak Farm in his own car while Basil and Barbara left separately, and Ann gave her father a lift back over to Vaulty Farm.

Ann then headed back home to Oak Farm, and it was only now that she, David and Peter examined the silencer once again. It was at this point that David realised that the red/brown substance on the silencer was, or could be, blood; they were sufficiently worried to call their cousin Anthony for advice, who suggested that they wrap it up for safekeeping, following which David wrapped it in a plastic bag and placed it in a wardrobe. It was now starting to dawn on them the implications of what they had found. If what they believed they had discovered was correct, then it implied that a silencer had been used during the murders. And if this was true, then Sheila categorically could not have killed herself by simple matter of the fact that she would have had to shoot herself, remove the silencer, head downstairs to store it in the cupboard and then head back upstairs to lie down on the floor and die. It seemed improbable at best.

The silencer is often cited as the most contentious piece of evidence in this case, partly because it was so potentially damning to Jeremy and yet its handling and journey from White House Farm to the laboratory where it was eventually tested was at best sloppy and at worst incompetent. David asserted that they 'rang the police immediately'[3] following the discovery but that it was up to three days later before the police collected it. Later he changed his statement saying that they had not informed the police straight away but that 'the silencer was left with Ann and I presumed she would phone the police.'[4] Ann maintained that she called the police that evening. The fact of the matter is that it was Robert Boutflour who eventually alerted Stan Jones to the discovery of the silencer on Monday 12 August while the police officer was there for the purposes of interviewing his wife, Pamela. On hearing the news Stan Jones headed over to Oak Farm to pick up the vital piece of evidence; he had no gloves with which to handle it securely but said he used a handkerchief to deposit it into a makeshift container consisting of a kitchen roll tube with a peg at either end. Before this however, he maintained he also saw the blood on the silencer and also, for the first time, a grey hair.

What happened next, if true, places a further shadow over the handling of this evidence as Stan Jones, far from heading immediately to Witham Police Station to hand over the evidence, accepted Peter's offer of a drink and, according to him, the men shared a glass of whisky before he headed off. Jeremy's supporters maintain that the officer shared not a glass but sunk a whole bottle before, much to Peter's alarm, driving off to deposit the silencer. They went on to allege far more issues with the silencer evidence but if true, this does bolster the idea that the collection of evidence was sloppy to say the least.

Stan did however take the silencer to Witham Police Station where he popped it in his desk drawer ready to hand to Miller the following morning who then handed it to Cook. He didn't feel the need to note it in the property register assuming it would 'go into the scenes of crime system and [be] recorded in that fashion.'[5] Cook collected the silencer at around 9.15 am on Tuesday 13 August and in turn took it to the laboratory to be processed, not before he and Miller had both visually assessed the item during which they agree that they also saw what appeared to be a grey hair attached to it. On arrival at the laboratory however, despite taping up the open end of the tube before transporting it, the hair had disappeared and so by the time he handed it over to biologist Glynis Howard for analysis, it was gone.

On examination, Howard identified four potential bloodstains on the silencer, and she took samples from two. While the family had to wait for the official results of the tests, they were now firmly of the opinion that Sheila could not possibly have shot herself; the discovery of the silencer further compounded their disbelief that Sheila could have carried out the murders coupled with the evidence that her feet were clean and her nails unbroken and the slightly more damning evidence that she was found to have not one but two gunshots in her neck.

Back at White House Farm during the visit where the silencer was found, Ann and Robert were also concerned by some other things they discovered that day. While starting her clean-up of the kitchen, Ann saw smudges and what she described as a diluted blood stain on the kitchen window which she and her father Robert ascertained could be closed from the outside by banging it to drop the interior latch, thus making it look as though it was locked from the inside. During his search of the house Robert also discovered several other entry and exit points which he felt an intruder could have used in the same way. Again, the idea of someone being able to pretend that the house was locked up from the inside while successfully being able to make their escape was still pure speculation on their part at this stage but further fuelled their mounting suspicions that Jeremy was somehow involved.

On the same day, Ann discovered June's missing bicycle at Jeremy's cottage in Goldhanger. She had been puzzling about it for a while since she hadn't been able to locate it at White House Farm and on realising it was in Goldhanger it further firmed up her fears that Jeremy had used it as a means of getting to and from White House Farm without being seen. Jeremy simply said he borrowed the bike to lend to Julie for her to get to work. By now, Ann and her father Robert had independently begun to keep a journal about their discoveries, and it was the contents of Robert's which some say influenced the police in forming a hypothesis of what occurred that evening. He had come to imagine that Jeremy had worn a wetsuit while committing the murders in order to keep himself clean and had cycled to and from the scene on June's bicycle.

Not only did the family now believe that Sheila could not have killed herself, but they were also beginning to suspect that Nevill could not or would not have telephoned Jeremy at just gone 3.00 am to tell him that his sister had gone berserk with a gun and evidence would soon become apparent to compound this theory. On 23 August Jeremy asked Barbara Wilson and Jean Boutell to help him clear out the farmhouse and on doing so, they found a fawn coloured Statesman telephone wrapped in its own cord tucked away amongst some magazines. This may not have been of great importance, but for the fact that the situation in White House Farm's pre-mobile phone era was usually consistent.

As a rule, the farmhouse contained four working phones. Downstairs, an Envoy cream cordless phone was usually kept in the kitchen but would often be used by Nevill in the nearby den. Also usually kept plugged in, in the kitchen was the Statesman digital handset. Upstairs, a digital Sceptre 100 was kept permanently on Nevill's desk in the office and in the master bedroom, an ivory rotary dial telephone was generally kept on Nevill's bedside table. If either of the phones in the kitchen were ever out of action, the rotary phone would invariably be taken downstairs to replace it.

On the night of the murders the cordless Envoy was not in the house; it was faulty and had been taken away on 5 August for repair. The crime scene photographs indicate that the Statesman phone was not in the kitchen and was evidently missing and had been replaced with the ivory rotary phone usually kept by Nevill's bedside. This means that during the attack there were only two phones readily accessible in the house; the Sceptre 100 in Nevill's office and the ivory rotary dial in the kitchen, the phone from which Nevill made the alleged phone call to Jeremy.

Barbara and Jean questioned Jeremy about the Statesman phone they found and were told it was a spare. When they plugged it in to test it and found it to be working perfectly, they were slightly perplexed as to why it had been coiled up and put out of the way. Again, faint alarm bells were ringing. Could someone have deliberately ensured there were no possible means of calling for help from the master bedroom by moving the rotary phone downstairs? Would it be easier to fake a phone being hung up on a rotary rather than a digital handset? Coupled with the result of the autopsies about the nature of Nevill's injuries appearing to conclude that he would not have been able to speak once downstairs, this began to shed a shadow of suspicion on Jeremy's claims that his father had placed a telephone call to him that night. And what could be the only possible explanation for him lying about this? That Jeremy had murdered his family and was creating himself an alibi.

Love Hurts

While this evidence was gradually being investigated and starting to gain traction with the police, a witness came forward who hammered the final nail in the coffin for Jeremy, and that person was his girlfriend, or perhaps by now ex-girlfriend, Julie Mugford.

In answer to the question of why Jeremy Bamber was arrested for and eventually convicted of murder, it could be argued that the catalyst for the most crucial developments in the case against him was Julie. The question of whether she was an innocent victim caught up in a web of deceit woven by her psychopathic boyfriend brought to the brink of despair by the weight of her knowledge and his torturous treatment of her, or simply a woman scorned looking for revenge against the man she had loved and lost is debated by those who think Jeremy is guilty, and those who think he has suffered the greatest miscarriage of justice in British history.

Given the background of infidelity, Jeremy and Julie's relationship was unlikely to flourish into old age, particularly when remembering that Jeremy was 24 and Julie just 21 when the murders happened. By any standards this was a very young age to be going through such an intense relationship anyway, never mind throwing in a family massacre. Notwithstanding Jeremy's alleged history with past girlfriends, it's likely they were both still relatively inexperienced and naïve when it came to the kind of sensible, mature decision making which can only develop from age and experience.

Did Jeremy treat Julie badly during their relationship? It's hard to deny that sometimes yes, he did. Do some hold the misogynistic view that she somehow deserved it? Absolutely. Jeremy's supporters have been known to criticise her clinginess and desperation and even the fact that she didn't like to cook but preferred to eat out in restaurants as reasons why Jeremy was justified in his treatment of her. Again, she was 21 years old, and thought she was in love.

What with Jeremy's somewhat unsettling behaviour, unsavoury arguments about money and inheritance and the unnerving discovery of potentially damning evidence, the weeks following the murders were turbulent at best for the family. Arguably, they had been made more so by the arrival of Jeremy's friend, Brett Collins who was certainly not welcomed with open arms by Julie. Her relationship with Jeremy was already starting to falter despite her attempts to keep it alive, and Brett's arrival did nothing whatsoever to help it.

Jeremy and Brett had met in 1982 in Brett's home country of New Zealand and having already visited Jeremy in Essex earlier in 1985 Brett had then gone on holiday to the Greek Islands and was there when the murders occurred, so on hearing the news he headed straight back to support his friend. Interestingly, Brett Collins has undergone a change of heart in the years following Jeremy's conviction for murder and has been vocal in interviews and documentaries about the case. He's keen now to paint a negative picture of his former friend, alleging that Jeremy lost the £5,000 diving money his father had gifted him to an errant heroin dealer and went on to sell some diamonds he'd brought with him to New Zealand, having stolen them from his grandmother. He's even gone on record to say he is convinced of Jeremy's guilt but thinks that he would have paid someone else to commit the act rather than resort to doing the deed himself.

Back in 1985 however, they were still firm friends, and perhaps due to the speculations about their sexuality their closeness did appear to drive a further wedge between Julie and Jeremy. When he arrived, Brett ploughed in with firm confidence in his friendship with Jeremy and appeared to join in with the pile-in whenever Jeremy took it upon himself to degrade Julie in public, even joining in when he made fun of her for looking pregnant at the funeral, presumably in some misguided attempt at a joke about her weight. Brett later claimed that Julie suspected a 'bromance' between the two men which caused a lot of friction between the three of them, not least because Jeremy clearly enjoyed Brett's company, perhaps by this stage much more so than he enjoyed Julie's.

Events seemed to be getting on top of her and less than two weeks after the funerals, on 29 August she broke down in front of her flat mate, Susan Battersby with whom she shared the flat in Caterham Road. She became more and more agitated until she finally felt compelled to let it all out, telling Susan 'You don't know how evil Jeremy is!'[1] She then proceeded to regale her flatmate with an extraordinary story told to her, by Jeremy, that he had been planning to kill his entire family for months, if not years.

He hadn't done the deed himself, she said, but had instead hired his former friend Matthew McDonald to kill his entire family for the princely sum of £2,000 (which at the time of writing equates to around £6,000). He had prepared the amateur hitman by giving him directions on how to enter and leave the farmhouse, explained exactly where he would leave the gun and accompanying ammunition and of course, told him to wear a mask to avoid detection. After committing the murders, Matthew reportedly told Jeremy he had shot the twins first, followed by Nevill who he had to fight to subdue, followed by June. He had then managed to persuade Sheila to 'calmly and without any arguments'[2] fake her own suicide by shooting herself. Finally, he called Jeremy on the phone from inside White House Farm to ensure that the last number dialled would corroborate Jeremy's story, and then exited the house via the window which could then be closed from the outside, as instructed.

When Julie had finished telling her this tale, Susan expressed surprise that Julie not already gone straight to the police with this news, Julie explained that Jeremy had threatened her with the suggestion that not only would the police 'laugh in her face'[3] at the allegations, but that she would then also be implicated in the crime. She was terrified. And she still loved him. A couple of days following the revelation, on 31 August, Jeremy and Julie finally broke up.

Their relationship appears to have been a litany of disappointments for Julie, perpetrated by Jeremy in the form of a stream of broken promises. This day was much the same; Julie had been expecting him at her flat as promised, but he had spent the day instead with Brett, and with one of his ex-girlfriends, Virginia Greaves who was, apparently, interested in renting Sheila's flat. Jeremy did eventually show up in the evening to take her out for a meal at Blazes restaurant in Blackheath. Only Jeremy and Julie know exactly what was said that night, but Julie claimed they discussed the murders, with her trying to establish just exactly what part he had played in them, if any. She also asked him if he still loved her. They say that you should never ask a question you are not prepared to hear the answer to, and the answer Julie got was lukewarm at best. He was unable to give her a definitive reply which was tantamount to saying no, he did not.

No matter how young or naïve Julie may have been she cannot have failed to take this hint and by the time they arrived back at her flat they had begun the well-worn, protracted process of an emotional break-up where one party is desperate to leave, and the other is desperate for them to stay. Julie remembers an emotionally driven tear fest. She admitted to, at one point, putting a pillow over Jeremy's head, with no real intention of killing him, but in the desperate panic of a 21-year-old who doesn't want her boyfriend to leave her. She admitted in her statement that she told Jeremy she had done it because 'if he were dead, he would always be with me.'[4] As expected, Jeremy's version is rather simpler; he says she begged him for 'one last shag'[5] after which he attempted to leave, hampered only by not being able to find his car keys.

The following morning, Julie confided in her friend Liz Rimmington the same story she had told Susan the previous week.

The timing of this is, to some, pertinent due to the fact that just before Julie's revelation to Liz, she had her own confession to make to Julie; that she had previously slept with Jeremy. For some this resulted in a furious Julie making up lies about Jeremy, although Liz denied ever telling Julie about the fling. Either way, after unburdening to both Susan and Liz, Julie was apparently still desperate to tell people the truth about Jeremy and the murders at White House Farm. On 2 September she called her friend Karen Bishop in distress and while she didn't come out with the full story, she heavily hinted that Jeremy was involved in the murders, branding him a psychopath.

However, Julie and Jeremy's relationship was still not quite over. On 4 September they had arranged to meet at Sheila's flat, with Julie wanting to talk more about the breakdown of their relationship and ascertain whether it was truly over or not. Brett was inevitably present, and during their talk Jeremy took a call from Virginia, sparking an angry outburst from Julie who took a Chinese box of Jeremy's and threw it against a mirror, smashing it and the box to pieces. Again, and understandably, their version of events differs, with Julie describing a scene in which she slapped Jeremy's face, and him retaliating by twisting her arm behind her back, prompting her to threaten to go to the police as Brett entered the room to see what all the commotion was about.

Jeremy's version is again calmer; he heard a noise, came to see if she was ok and they calmly discussed Virginia, and Julie then left. Interestingly, given the acrimonious break-up, Jeremy held good to his word on an offer to help her move house a few days later. As Julie recalled, 'we left on a reasonably happy note. I haven't seen him since.'[6] However, she was clearly still distraught and Liz, understandably concerned about what she had been told, persuaded Julie on 7 September to tell her boyfriend, Malcolm what she had previously revealed about Jeremy being involved in the murders. She agreed and finally, at 4.00 pm that day, Liz phoned Witham police station, sending a message to Stan Jones that Julie was ready to talk to him.

From here things moved quickly; Julie's statement given to Stan Jones and Miller that evening took around three-and-a-half hours, following which Stan Jones contacted Chief Superintendent Harris who in turn passed him on to Detective Superintendent Mike Ainsley to update him on the developments. He, accompanied by Taff Jones, headed to the station and by 11.00 pm were in the interview room with Julie. By the end of the interview, Ainsley said that he 'realised that I was listening to the horrific truth.'[7] The culmination of Julie's various statements taken that night and over the forthcoming weeks essentially formed the following sequence of events:

Jeremy had first mentioned his plans around seven months after he and Julie began dating, sometime between July and October 1984. At this stage the talk consisted of hating his family and his general feeling of entitlement, he felt they were not doing enough for him and he wished they were dead. This developed into the formation of plans as to how he could put this into action and make it a reality, justifying potential murder by explaining that he would be putting his crazy sister out of her misery, and saving the boys from a life of growing up 'disturbed.' Colin, he reasoned, would be pleased to be rid of the 'millstone around his neck',[8] his beloved twin sons.

Jeremy's first plan was to drug the entire family with sleeping pills and then set fire to the house, which he quickly dismissed as it had too many potential flaws. He wondered then about the same plan but with an attempt to make it look as though his father had fallen asleep in his chair in the den, accidentally setting fire to the house. At this stage he introduced the idea of leaving the house, having said goodbye to the occupants, and then returning by means of walking or cycling the back way, knowing there was a way of entering and leaving the farmhouse while making it look as though everything was locked up from the inside.

Julie almost became inadvertently caught up in the plan, she says, when she mentioned some Temazepam tablets she had been prescribed for insomnia; Jeremy 'for one reason or another had it in his mind that I had bought the pills especially for him so he could use them on his parents' but he soon ditched this plan when he tested them on himself and they seemed to have no useful effect. A few months later he began developing another plan having ditched the idea of drugs being involved, albeit briefly dallying with the idea of trying to get hold of some cyanide, and eventually also mooting the idea of a fire as it would demolish too many valuable items. He finally rested upon the idea of Sheila as a scapegoat due to her mental health issues, going so far as to plan the telephone call from White House Farm to his number in Goldhanger to back up his story. Honing the plan, he did a trial run to check the cycle ride would take fifteen minutes one way and told Julie that the entire household would be shot, following which he would let himself out of the window with the faulty latch. She said that this plan was formed in July, but that he didn't mention it to her again until the day before the murders, on 6 August 1985.

Julie tells a different story to that which Jeremy put forward in terms of his phone calls to her on that night. He said that he called her after speaking to Chelmsford Police Station to tell her that something was happening at the farm and again at 5.40 am to say that a police car would be coming to get her. Julie insisted she'd received another phone call on the day before the murders took place, in which Jeremy told her that he had 'been thinking on the tractor and the crime will have to be tonight or never.'[9] This took place at around 10.00 pm and Julie had been smoking a joint so was not fully alert and therefore dismissed what he'd said and told him not to be so stupid. It was only when she woke in the night that she realised what he may have meant by his words. The call she took in the early hours was, she says, made in order for Jeremy to let her know that everything was going to plan and he told her that 'everything is going well, not to worry, there is something wrong at the farm' followed by 'bye honey, I love you lots.'[10] The timing of this call is, if not crucial, certainly telling of Jeremy's motivation that night. Julie called on her flatmates for help with when it had occurred; one friend who had been staying with them recalled that it had come in at around 3.00 am and Susan Battersby remembered that she had looked at her clock as it did, which displayed 3.12 am. Either way, the implication is that Jeremy chose to call her *before* calling the police. He rang again at 5.40 am, as witnessed by Police Constable Lay, to briefly warn her that a police car would be coming to pick her up.

Later, at Bourtree Cottage, Stan Jones's assertion that he heard a chuckle or laugh coming from the room where Jeremy and Sheila were talking is borne out by Julie's version of events; when they were finally alone, she says, Jeremy leaned in close, laughing and whispering in her ear that 'I should have been an actor'[11] following which the giggling couple were interrupted by Stan Jones's arrival when he saw the pair break away from each other. It was on that same day, after everyone had finally left the cottage that Julie said she confronted Jeremy to ask if he had done it and it was at this point that he said no but pointed the finger at their friend Matthew McDonald.

Following Julie's long interview with the police, a couple of days later on 9 September, Christine Bacon, Matthew's girlfriend was taken into custody at 6.30 am but was unable to help much apart from confirming that there wasn't a lot of love lost between Jeremy and his parents. Matthew had no idea that she was in custody and on letting himself into her flat that evening he was faced with Collins and Delgado who arrested him on suspicion of committing offences against the firearms act. During his interview he admitted that on the night of the murders he was with neither his wife or Christine but had in fact been with an entirely different woman which was eventually substantiated. Following a prolonged interview which lasted until 12 September, the police were finally confident that Matthew McDonald was not involved in the murders at White House Farm.

On the face of it, the fact that Julie pointed the finger at Matthew who then appeared to have a solid alibi implies that she was lying.

However, perhaps another way of looking at it was that she blamed Matthew McDonald because she truly believed he was responsible. Why did she believe it? Because this was the story which Jeremy put to her. Perhaps he did so as some sort of insurance; in the event that Julie turned against him and went to the police, she would be disbelieved after spouting a tale he knew could be disproven, therefore making Julie out to be the liar, not him.

Mistakes Had Been Made

Meanwhile, on Sunday 8 September and as a result of Julie's revelations, Taff Jones headed over to the Maida Vale flat to pick up Jeremy and bring him in for questioning. Although it's clear that Taff Jones was still not convinced of Jeremy's potential guilt, it would have been foolish not to pursue this new evidence and hence Jeremy found himself being cautioned and interviewed by the detective. According to one source, a total of nine officers attended the flat to pick him up: Jones himself, alongside Miller, Barlow, three uniformed officers, a SOCO and two CID officers. Brett Collins was apparently firmly linked by this point; as he emerged from the twins' bedroom where he had been sleeping naked, he too was taken in for questioning as by association he was also wanted in connection with the murders.

While Taff Jones interviewed Jeremy and Miller did the honours with Brett, Stan Jones learned that Jeremy had been brought in and was, apparently, furious that he hadn't been in attendance when it happened. Perhaps understandably he felt that it was his perseverance which had led the police to this state of affairs, and things didn't look as though they would improve for him any time soon; while he was concurrently continuing his interview with Julie, Jeremy was meanwhile denying absolutely everything to Taff Jones, who was getting nowhere fast and becoming more and more convinced that Jeremy was not their man, and that Julie was lying.

Perhaps due to this lack of progress, shortly afterwards Detective Superintendent Mike Ainsley was asked by Assistant Chief Constable Peter Simpson to replace Taff Jones as senior investigating officer (SIO) with immediate effect, although according to a television interview he suggests that there 'hadn't really been an SIO'[1] before then as Essex Police hadn't believed that there was anything to investigate. In fact, years later he would make it clear that he was not at all impressed by the police work which had preceded him. 'Mistakes had been made. Let me explain to you. The officers who attended the scene included a CSI who had been a DSI for 14 years, a DCI, police surgeon and a number of lesser ranked officers. They were taken in completely by what appeared to be Bamber's concern for his family. Bamber made them believe what he wanted them to believe. I'm not saying I would have done any different, I don't know. But I do know that looking at it afterwards I can see where all the faults were.'[2]

Following his appointment Ainsley swiftly established a major incident office named Operation Raleigh and essentially reopened the case, changing the status of the investigation from one of murder-suicide to simply murder. Events now began to progress rather swiftly, if not before time and he headed to Vaulty Manor to deliver the news to Robert Boutflour that his nephew had been arrested for the murder of June, Nevill, Sheila, Daniel and Nicholas.

Next, Ainsley set into motion what should have been done immediately following the discovery of the bodies (whether the cause was assumed to involve suicide or not); a full scene of crime and scientific search of both White House Farm and Bourtree Cottage. The farm underwent an extensive fingerprint examination, searches for traces of blood, and inspections for entry and exit marks, while Jeremy's clothing was also carefully examined. Cook headed up the investigation at Jeremy's home at Bourtree Cottage where the house and Jeremy's Vauxhall Astra were also searched.

On 9 September, during a case conference headed by Simpson, the attendees were asked one by one what their thoughts were on this latest turn of events; Stan Jones reiterated that he had believed Jeremy to be guilty from the beginning while his counterpart Taff Jones insisted that his original theory that it was a murder-suicide still stood. Divisional Superintendent George Harris was convinced by the former's argument, as was Simpson and they agreed for the time being to formally charge Jeremy with the burglary at Osea Road. Ainsley later recalled that they wanted him on remand for that offence so that he could get on with investigating the murder aspect. However, he said he 'did not anticipate him confessing to anything.'[3]

By 10 September, Stan Jones finally got his chance to interview Jeremy, in the presence of his solicitor Bruce Bowler and accompanied by Clark. Stan headed into this with gusto and optimism, convinced that he would be able to wring a confession out of his prisoner, but he would ultimately be disappointed in this regard. The questioning, which would go on to last three days, focused mainly on Jeremy's relationship with Julie Mugford and despite his apparent calm it was during this interrogation that he 'got himself in a muddle with the timings of the calls, and what he had told Taff Jones previously.'[4] In his original statement taken on 7 August he stated his father had called him at 3.10 am following which he called the police, then calling Julie at around 3.25 am. During his interview with Stan Jones, he firstly admitted to calling Julie before calling the police, but that he didn't 'remember my reasons' why. On being challenged on this point, he said that his first statement must have been correct and on being asked to confirm if he had in fact called the police first, agreed 'that must be the case' and that his assertion just now that his call to Julie had been placed first was a 'mistake.'[5] He had, however, on the first day of his interview told Jones that he had called Julie first; he was clearly confused on the point.

Towards the end of this interview, on 12 September Jeremy was challenged with the Matthew McDonald story which he refuted in its entirety. Having no evidence with which to hold him for the murders, on 13 September he was driven to the magistrate's court in Chelmsford and charged with the Osea Road theft. Following this, Essex Police had no choice but to release him on bail and order him to come back to face the charges on 16 October. For now, he was free. He wasted no time, and by all accounts headed straight into London with Brett, who had already been released without charge, where they allegedly partied with Virginia Greaves and her sister Anji.

Three days later proved to be a busy day for Jeremy; on 16 September he informed his solicitor that he was planning to go abroad for a break, but not before meeting with The Sun journalist Michael Fielder that same day to allegedly ask for £20,000 in return for the nude pictures he possessed of Sheila. In a rare show of humanity, the newspaper refused them, but still managed to get their scoop with the following day's headline proclaiming 'Bambi Brother in Photo Scandal'[6] instead. While Brett is alleged to have been instrumental in setting up the meeting, he later claimed that he has no recollection of the event and Jeremy of course now denies it happened at all, although at the time his reaction to the accusation was simply that he hadn't read the papers yet so would be unable to comment on what might be on the front page that day. It's unclear how many photographs of this type existed, as later Jeremy's supporters claimed they 'didn't exist'[7] at this point, due to Jeremy already having handed them over to Colin a week or so previously.

Later that day he snuck into White House Farm to retrieve his passport before heading to the South of France with Brett which again would later be viewed with suspicion and perhaps contention; was this proof that he was able to get in and out of a locked White House Farm, or was he doing this to place any trace of himself quite openly in the window there, should anything occur to throw suspicion on him later on? While Jeremy and Brett were abroad, the case seemed to explode in the press; the papers were full of stories, now imagining a drug connection with the murders with stories of light planes flying overhead and drug dropping zones in the farm grounds. Some of the content must have been leaked which understandably embarrassed

Essex Police who were by this stage somewhat ashamed of the way the investigation was going, especially under the press accusation that they just couldn't make up their minds in which direction to take it. Local residents, at this point, were saying that they had always known that Sheila had not been responsible for the crimes and were not at all surprised that the finger of blame now appeared to be hovering towards her brother.

In the meantime, the detectives were ploughing their way through thousands of transcripts, despite Taff Jones's continued insistence that they were after the wrong man. However, by now the renewed investigation was in full swing and despite Stan Jones's trepidation about the lack of evidence they had so far managed to uncover, they delivered their initial findings to the Director of Public Prosecutions (DPP), the predecessor to the current Crown Prosecution Service (CPS), and were somewhat taken aback to be given the go ahead to arrest and charge Jeremy with the murders of his family.

Despite this upturn in their favour, they now found themselves in a quandary; Jeremy was still abroad, and they had no idea when he was planning to return, having discovered from the travel agent through which he'd bought the tickets that they were open ended and with no return specified. Special Branch however were on the case, and on 29 September they called to inform Essex Police that Jeremy and Brett had been detained on their arrival at customs in Dover, where they had just arrived back from their holiday in France.

Stan Jones would have his moment after all; it was he who made the long drive there accompanied by Clark and Miller to meet Jeremy Bamber in what he later described as a 'disappointing arrest.'[8] Jeremy's reaction to being informed that he was being detained on suspicion of murder was a simple 'ok' and during the two-hour trip back to Essex, the conversation rarely deviated from him talking about his holiday. He was calm personified. Jeremy Bamber was formally charged with the murder of his family at 10.15 pm on 29 September 1985, fifty-three days after their deaths, at the police headquarters in Chelmsford with Bruce Bowler, his solicitor in attendance. The following day at Maldon Magistrate's Court he quietly confirmed that he understood the charges against him. This time, he was not awarded bail.

TRIAL

I could Kill Anybody. I could Even Kill my Parents

Things moved swiftly thereafter; on 7 November 1985 Ainsley submitted his final report to the DPP, fully setting out the case that the Essex Police wished to present in court and by early 1986 Jeremy was housed in Brixton Prison and the prosecution and defence began to prepare for trial. Jeremy was by now represented by Geoffrey Rivlin QC as lead counsel with Edmund Lawson QC as junior. However, while they did not exactly concede defeat, even his own team warned Jeremy before trial they felt there were issues with proving the plausibility of Sheila having committed the murders with these concerns mostly being centred, unsurprisingly, around the alleged blood on the silencer. In another potential blow from within his own team, the psychiatrist they hired concluded that Jeremy not only displayed psychopathic traits but that 'if ever there was a psychopath, it's Jeremy Bamber.'[1] His theory was that Jeremy was not necessarily lying about being innocent, but that he might be guilty and had been able to successfully repress the knowledge of what he had done. Not the result they were after perhaps, but still not necessarily *proof* of guilt.

Further drama followed; in May 1986 Taff Jones tragically died in a freak accident at his home when a stepladder he was using broke, causing him to fall and fracture his skull. With that he lost forever the chance to give evidence or indeed witness the outcome of the trial of the man whose innocence he maintained throughout the investigation, although whether or not his input would have had any influence on the verdict is of course impossible to tell. Given the outcome of the enquiry which took place after the verdict, it is perhaps unlikely that it would have made very much difference at all.

The much-anticipated trial began at Chelmsford Crown Court on 2 October 1986 presided over by Justice Maurice Drake in front of a jury of seven men and five women with the prosecution led by Anthony Arlidge QC. During his opening speech, the barrister seemed to concede right from the beginning that this was certainly no open and shut case and indeed the idea of Sheila committing the murders was at the very least plausible but countered with the evidence of Jeremy's behaviour and the blood on the silencer which, he asserted, told a different story altogether to the one put forward by the defence.

While it was clear that this blood would be key, alongside the red paint found on the silencer which had since been proven to match scratches on the kitchen AGA, the prosecution's full list of evidence they intended to show throughout the trial was extensive if not largely circumstantial. There was Jeremy's expressed dislike of his family and his confession to Julie of his plans to kill them. There was the bike discovered at Goldhanger; proof that it had been used by Jeremy as a possible getaway vehicle and his admission that he was able to enter and leave the building without any trace.

There was Nevill's phone call; the evidence proved it never happened by virtue of there being no blood discovered on the handset and they could prove that he had been injured upstairs, proving it impossible for him to have spoken on the phone downstairs. Behaviourally, in this set of circumstances they believed Nevill would have called the police directly or that Jeremy would have called 999 immediately. At the very least, they would have expected him to alert the farm workers nearby and head to the farm at speed had Sheila actually gone on a rampage with a gun.

The fundamental basis of the prosecution's case, however, was the fact that, given the events of the night, there could only be two possible suspects: Sheila and Jeremy. Therefore, the burden on the prosecution would be to a) disprove Sheila as a credible suspect and b) prove the opposite of Jeremy. There seemed to be more evidence to disprove Sheila as a credible suspect than the other way round and it was mainly derived of physical evidence surrounding Sheila herself. She was not thought to be physically capable of overpowering Nevill, her hands and feet were clean when she was found, indicating that she hadn't walked around in blood, there was no evidence from swabs that she had loaded and reloaded a gun, and her long fingernails were intact and unchipped.

There was also evidence surrounding the gun and silencer; this contained traces of Sheila's blood, could not have been removed by Sheila after she had shot herself, and would have made it impossible for her to fit the gun under her chin and then shoot herself. Evidence about Sheila's mental health was also raised; she had not deteriorated in the days leading up to the murders or expressed any suicidal thoughts, and apart from Jeremy, no-one had ever seen her use a gun. Due to her poor co-ordination, she would not have been capable of loading and operating the rifle, Arlidge said.

Evidence against Jeremy was concise and both physical and behavioural, centred generally around the alleged phone call from Nevill but last and certainly not least Arlidge told the jury that Jeremy stood to inherit a small fortune on the death of his entire family; one of the oldest motives known to man and the court of law.

During the presentation of the prosecution's case many witnesses were called, inevitably including several officers involved in the events; Police Constable Michael West and civilian Malcolm Bonnet gave evidence about the timings of the calls made by Jeremy on 7 August. While at this stage they were unaware of the significance it might have in Jeremy's later appeals, at this point the prosecution was focussing on the times in an attempt to establish who Jeremy had called first; was it the police, or was it Julie?

Even during their testimonies there was confusion; West firstly confirmed that the time he received Jeremy's call he had himself recorded on the log as 3.36 am, by use of a digital clock on the wall of the station. While Jeremy was still on the line, he then contacted the headquarters information room to find out which station would cover the area of White House Farm. When told it was Witham, he then 'spoke to an officer on the personal radio link.' He then returned to Jeremy after what he estimated to be around three minutes, who remarked 'Christ, you've been a long time.'[2] He then told Jeremy to proceed to the farm, tried to ring the farm himself, and made contact with British Telecom at 3.42 am to check to see if the line was engaged or off the hook.

In cross examination by the defence, he was asked if it was possible that he had mistaken the time of the call, to which he agreed, in that he said he had since been informed that he spoke to the information room earlier than he had recorded, and so he must have written the time down incorrectly. He confirmed that 'there is certainly a dispute over the times. I don't know whose time is right and whose time is wrong.'[3] Overall, he estimated that he had spent around one minute initially talking to Jeremy, then another three minutes calling the information room and then Witham, before returning to Jeremy.

It was towards the end of his cross examination that West confirmed that while Rivlin was currently referring to a statement made by him on 13 September, he had also made a previous statement of which the defence were unaware. The statement was duly presented and was found to contain the statement that 'at about 3.26 on Wednesday 7th I was on duty when I received an exchange phone call.'[4] At this stage, the defence were interested in whether or not Jeremy had by this time claimed to have called Witham Police Station himself, which West confirmed he said he had, presumably in the hope that if this was not confirmed, that it would throw doubt on the fact that he had allegedly called Julie at 3.15 am *before* calling Witham. Malcolm Bonnett took the stand to confirm that he had been contacted by West at 3.26 am and hence despatched the first car at 3.35 am, confirming that Jeremy's initial contact must have been before 3.26 am.

Sergeant Chris Bews testified that the possible sighting of someone in the window was a trick of the light and Police Constable Stephen Myall recalled that Jeremy had seemed well dressed for that time of the morning. Firearms team leader Sergeant Douglas Adams and Dr Ian Craig both testified that it was virtually impossible to establish what time any of the victims had died.

Detective Constable David Bird and Detective Inspector Ron Cook were both called in respect of the treatment of the crime scene; Bird confirmed he had taken photos at the crime scene and that Sheila's hands had been moved in order for him to photograph the bloodstain on her nightdress and Cook confirmed that he was the one responsible for moving her hand and for ensuring that the gun was moved away from Sheila's body after she, and it, had been photographed. He also confirmed that the gun was checked by a firearms officer as it was moved, given a safety check and then leant against the wall. Cook testified about the loss of the grey hair which had allegedly been attached to the silencer, during which he was admonished by Mr Justice Drake that the staff at the laboratory should have been told of its existence whether it was lost or not, which did not happen.

It was during the evidence given by these officers that the prosecution ascertained that no-one had made a detailed search of the cupboard where the silencer was later found. Sergeant Woodcock confirmed that he didn't notice the silencer when he was carrying out his initial search but also that it wouldn't have been of interest even if they had, as they were not at that stage looking for evidence of a murderer.

Then followed the main exhibit, with forensic evidence given concerning the blood belonging to Sheila on the silencer, and speculation that the grey hair could have belonged to Nevill although this was really a moot point, given that he was a resident in the house and the hair in question had been lost. Dr Vanezis outlined the evidence surrounding the wounds on the victims and while he conceded that he couldn't confirm one way or another if Sheila's were a result of suicide, there was no evidence on her body that she had tried to fight anyone off. However, Malcolm Fletcher gave ballistic evidence of backspatter, a blood pattern which occurs when 'blood is projected backwards relative to the direction of a force'[5] which indicated away from suicide.

Clearly their case was going to rely heavily on behaviour; either focussing on Jeremy's alleged suspicious actions or establishing that Sheila had not been behaving like a crazed murderer in the days leading up to the murders. James Richards, a friend of Julie Mugford's, testified to having heard Jeremy state several times that 'I hate my fucking parents'[6] and later, Robert Boutflour testified that he had heard Jeremy once state that 'I could kill anybody, I could even kill my parents.'[7] Liz Rimington confirmed that he had bragged about getting a Porsche in an echo of his conversation with police on the night of the murder.

The Foakes family were called; Len, Dorothy and their daughter Julie who all agreed that Sheila was a happy and loving mother whose demeanour had not changed in the days before the murders, also testifying that Jeremy had once told them that he had no intention of sharing his inheritance with Sheila, and that if anything ever happened to his family his plan would be to sell up. Jean Boutell and Barbara Wilson each spoke of believing that Sheila's illness had if anything seemed better in the days and weeks preceding the murders, and that Nevill had not been himself the night before the murders. Dr Ann Wilkinson confirmed that Sheila's Haloperidol prescription had been reduced from 200mg to 100mg not long before the murders took place, so that the last dose Sheila was given would have been a 100mg one.

The family's evidence proved controversial. June's sister Pamela Boutflour confirmed that Sheila had no practical knowledge of or experience in the use of guns, and David, Ann, Peter, Robert and

Anthony, all corroborated one another on the discovery of the silencer. Anthony confirmed that when he had last visited the farm before the murders the .22 rifle had been situated in the gun cupboard with the silencer and scope still attached. Ann's testimony was apparently fractious as she reported that she had been troubled right from the start when Jeremy made his statement. When Robert was testifying, he became agitated at the suggestion that he may have cut himself and got his own blood on the silencer. Colin later said that the family's testimony worried him; such was their glaringly obvious animosity towards Jeremy that he was afraid the jury might turn against them in favour of the downtrodden defendant. His own testimony consisted mainly of his confirmation that Sheila was loving towards her children and that he believed she would never have hurt them.

The star witness was, without doubt, Julie Mugford and her evidence regarding the alleged phone calls between herself and Jeremy was vital. Alongside retelling the events leading up to the murder that she had put forward to the police she testified that, on the night of the murders Jeremy had called her at 10.00 pm during which he told her 'the crime will have to be tonight or never.'[8] She had received a second call at some time between 3.00 am and 3.20 am during which he told her that 'everything is going well, not to worry, there is something wrong at the farm'[9] and again at 5.40 am when he had called her to tell her that a police car was on its way to fetch her.

In cross examination Rivlin inevitably tried to undermine her testimony, highlighting his confusion as to why she didn't come forward with this evidence sooner, if not straight away and during her five hours in the witness box he called into question her reliability as an honest witness given her admission to being a part of the Osea Road burglary, cheque fraud, and her habitual use of marijuana. Julie's evidence was both emotional and controversial but, in the end, she held firm in what she had told officers right from the beginning.

Detective Sergeant Stan Jones corroborated her story that Jeremy had laughed and told her that he should have been an actor, given that he heard the chuckle at the same time as she said this occurred. Susan Battersby also corroborated Julie's account, confirming that she had 'told her Matthew McDonald had done it'[10] but both Matthew McDonald and his girlfriend Christine Bacon testified in rebuttal to those claims. Even Julie's mother, Mary Mugford was called as a witness, during which she testified that Jeremy had preferred her to his own mother, whom he professed to hate.

Do you believe Jeremy Bamber, or do you believe Julie Mugford?

In retaliation, the defence, led by Geoffrey Rivlin QC, countered with a similar if opposite case; to prove Sheila guilty and therefore Jeremy innocent.

Rivlin's opening statement was of course in stark contrast to Arlidge's, focussing on Sheila's deteriorating mental health, her delusions about having been taken over by the devil and her intrusive thoughts about having sex with her sons, suggesting that her cannabis use may have exacerbated her psychosis. Evidently in response to the prosecution's star evidence in the form of the silencer, he suggested that the perpetrators of altruistic killings often indulge in ritualistic behaviour and given this fact, it was not unthinkable that Sheila may have cleaned herself up and put the silencer back in the cupboard before finally turning the gun on herself, taking into account her serious mental illness and the fact that she had expressed thoughts about killing her children previously. In terms of forensics, the ace up their sleeve was their claim that the blood discovered on the silencer could well have been a mixture of June and Nevill's, rendering the prosecution's case moot.

Rivlin asserted that Sheila did, in fact, know how to operate the rifle having been brought up on a farm, and that the perfect storm of an argument about childcare and a semi-loaded gun having been left within her reach led to the inevitable breakdown. He pointed out that no injuries had been found on Jeremy, or indeed any bloodstained clothing of his ever recovered, coupled with the fact that Dr Craig had initially believed Sheila had been guilty of the crimes based on the evidence he saw. To counter the arguments about Jeremy's actions he had not, he said, immediately realised the seriousness of the situation and so had not called 999. The prosecution was unable to produce any witnesses to Jeremy entering or leaving White House Farm on the night of the murders, nor seen him travel between there and his home in Goldhanger.

Furthermore, it seemed that the defence planned to target not only Julie but anyone else who spoke up against Jeremy. Rivlin promised to illustrate how badly flawed Julie's testimony was, prove she had lied simply so that, if she could not have Jeremy then no-one else could, and lastly as a sort of catch all, that the witnesses speaking up against Jeremy were either lying, or had misinterpreted his words.

On 16 October 1986, Jeremy took the stand. Described as self-composed and detached in stark contrast to his ex-girlfriend's emotional testimonial, this attitude seemed to have, if anything, a negative impact on the jury. His initial evidence, coaxed by Rivlin, was of course by its very nature calm and persuasive and designed to explain away everything alleged by the prosecution. Yes, of course he was experienced with guns, but so was his sister, albeit to a lesser extent. His relationship with her had been good, although he 'didn't understand her.' During his quiet, measured testimony he once again confirmed his view of his sister's mental health issues, claiming 'she wanted to be with God. She wanted to go to heaven.' Not only that, but 'she wanted to take people with her.' He also claimed he had 'personally witnessed Sheila punching one of her young children.'[1]

His relationship with his parents was very loving, he said, although he admitted that June's sometimes zealous religious beliefs occasionally 'caused some friction'[2] between them. In terms of the night of the murders, he confirmed his parents had raised the subject of having Daniel and Nicholas fostered but that Sheila didn't seem to be paying much attention.

When his father called him that night, he had 'not initially appreciated the seriousness of the situation when receiving the call from his father and then became frightened to attend the scene alone,' which explained away why he didn't immediately call 999. He countered Julie's testimony saying he had called her immediately *after* calling the police because he 'needed a friendly ear,' and that she 'thought the whole thing was a practical joke.' He had driven slowly to the scene as he was afraid of what he might find. As to what happened at the scene; had he or the police officers seen movement inside the house? 'We thought we saw something, and we ducked down behind a hedge'[3] he said. He made clear his frustration with the officers, claiming that he tried to explain Sheila's mental health issues but to no avail, and felt the police didn't understand what he was trying to get across.

During his cross examination he remained as calm as ever and continued with what appeared to be his defence team's plan of simply explaining away as lies, anything which contradicted his testimony. He did however admit that the motive for his part in the Osea Road burglary was 'partly greed' and that he had occasionally argued with his parents, although flatly denied James Richards's claims he said he 'fucking hated' them, again implying this had been a lie told out of loyalty to Julie.

However, on the following day as his cross examination continued, things became a bit more tense. Why would people lie about him, Arlidge asked, what would be their motive for doing so? The prosecution continued to drive home the idea of Jeremy's greed, and his fractious relationship with his family. However, for many, a turning point seemed to be when Jeremy was questioned about how sensible it had been for him to leave the loaded rifle where his sister would have full access. In an exchange that appeared to come across as arrogant on his part, Jeremy countered that 'I didn't know what was going to happen, did I?' When Arlidge put to him that, 'You're not telling the truth about it, are you?' he calmly replied, 'That is what you've got to try and establish.' According to Ainsley, at that point a 'low murmur went around the court' and, it was at this moment that he thought to himself 'you've just convicted yourself.'[4]

Compared to the prosecution, the defence did not call as many witnesses, and in fact some were notable by their absence; people who had previously spoken up in his defence but who did not appear included Sue Ford, Brett Collins and Virginia Greaves. However, by 20 October the focus of the defence was on the takedown of Sheila, with their main witness being Dr Ferguson, the consultant who had looked after both Sheila and her mother June.

He confirmed that Sheila was psychotic and had become extremely agitated, perhaps not helped by occasional cannabis and cocaine use. He testified that between 1983-1985 she had developed an obsession with her cervix and had experienced a psychotic episode in March 1985 during which she was 'more acutely disturbed, very agitated and highly suspicious and bewildered.' His testimony however didn't put Sheila in an altogether negative light; while he conceded she would have reacted 'very strongly' to any attempt at taking Daniel and Nicholas away from her, he also did not feel she had the capacity to be violent towards them, and that although she had on occasion expressed a desire to 'be with Jesus'[5] she didn't appear, to him, to be suicidal.

Professor Bernard Knight, a forensic pathologist, was also called to testify about ritualistic murders and suicides where he determined it would have been 'unlikely' for a third person to be able to kill Sheila by putting the gun up against her chin without her objecting.

Following the conclusion of the defence's case, the jury requested more information and clarification from the judge on the beneficiaries of June and Nevill's estate, asking the question 'If Jeremy Bamber was found guilty and imprisoned for many years, who would be the beneficiarys [sic] of the Bamber estate and monies. Could it be his uncle and family? A possible reason or motif [sic] from Robert

Boutflour's statement about Jeremy being able to kill his own parents.'[6] Through Basil Cock, they received the reply that in this scenario Jeremy would not inherit and that in fact civil proceedings might be needed to establish the correct distribution of the estate but in any case, any such inheritance would go to his wife Pamela, not directly to Uncle Robert.

In summing up for the prosecution, Arlidge once again reinforced the idea that this was a two-horse race between Jeremy and Sheila and that the evidence all pointed away from the latter being guilty. She was vacant rather than psychotic due to her reduced prescription, it was ridiculous that anyone could imagine her overpowering her strong father, and he put the lack of defensive wounds on her body down to her sheer paralysing terror during the attack. He dismissed Jeremy's excuse for not calling 999 as weak and was confident enough to posit that even without the silencer evidence, while key, their case was still strong. He ended with some harsh words to the jury; 'somebody in this case is lying and lying their heads off. Either Julie Mugford is lying, or Jeremy Bamber is lying. It is something you've got to face.'[7]

Rivlin, in defence, agreed to this statement although for them, it was Julie's performance of a testimony which was a tissue of lies. She could easily have got the information required to make her story sound convincing from the press, he said, and that she was a 'skilled actress or consummate actor' in doing so. Not only that, but it just didn't add up that Jeremy would have confessed all to her; why would he entrust her with such a dark secret? Their attempt to discredit Julie continued, once again bringing up her criminal past. Sheila's decline in mental health had been drastic, he said; the murders reeked of overkill followed by ritualistic cleansing.

Justice Drake's summing up began on Friday 24 October 1986 and has become contentious, with one anonymous juror later admitting that Drake's directing them to find Jeremy guilty was the turning point and, had it not happened, he believed they would have found

Jeremy not guilty. Indeed, the defence were furious at its contents which they found to be totally biased in favour of Jeremy's guilt. In it, Justice Drake confirmed to the jury that there was no third party involved here, either Jeremy was guilty, or Sheila was, but it was not for the defence to prove Sheila guilty but for the prosecution to prove she was a victim. He asked them; did they believe Julie's testimony had the ring of truth to it? If so, they should also bear in mind that she might have a possible motive to tell lies. Again, a question; was the silencer on the gun? Why on earth would Sheila go to the trouble of taking it off? The blood evidence, he said, could alone lead them to find Jeremy guilty, but they should also be able to set it aside and still do so. It should not be relied upon.

On Monday 27 October he took the jury through the entirety of Julie's testimony again, asking them to think carefully as to whether they considered it possible that it was a pack of lies, given that she had proven herself capable of repeating it over and over again. He went through the timings of the phone calls and reiterated that there was no evidence against Sheila other than that she was found in the house with the gun. There were no defensive wounds discovered on either Sheila or Jeremy but he also put forward the idea that the latter had time to clean himself up. In the end, he said 'quite simply, do you believe Jeremy Bamber, or do you believe Julie Mugford?'[8]

The jury left the courtroom at 12.49 pm but returned at 5.59 pm, with a request to hear the blood evidence again, in particular the chances of it belonging just to Sheila, or whether it might be a possible mix of June and Nevill's, following which Munday (in Arlidge's absence) and Rivlin privately presented the evidence to Justice Drake again which he then confirmed he understood. The jury were brought back in, so that he could in turn relay it to them, during which he made one small but important error, stating that Hayward was able to tell just by looking that the blood was singular and not mixed, which was not altogether correct.

Following this non-clarification the jury adjourned for another two-and-a-half hours before returning with the final verdict, having been given permission by Drake to settle for a majority rather than unanimous decision if necessary. Following the twenty-six-day trial, a ten-to-two majority jury answered Justice Drake's question as to who they believed, and it was Julie. Jeremy was found guilty on five counts of murder and sentenced to life imprisonment with a recommendation to serve a minimum of twenty-five years.

Matters of Pure Speculation

Essex Police Force were understandably elated at this result and didn't initially feel any further investigation or enquiry was necessary following the conviction but given that the Daily Mail went on to describe them as 'the Clouseau squad who let the evil murderer stay at large for too long'[1] it was only a matter of hours before the then Home Secretary Douglas Hurd called for a report into the case. A police enquiry was immediately launched into the circumstances surrounding the investigation and Jeremy's subsequent arrest, with the emphasis being not on whether it was the correct course of action, but rather why it had not been carried out sooner.

The internal review was led by Detective Chief Superintendent James Dickinson and culminated in a report more than 300 pages long, the gist of it being that it was unfortunate that the now late Taff Jones was unable to account for his decisions, as they were 'the focal point of accountability in respect of any inadequacies.'[2] The report at no point deemed these inadequacies to be intentional but were rather the result of mistaken judgment and honest actions. It contained plenty of other criticisms, particularly over the lack of structure but there was praise for the scene of crime photography and for Ainsley's subsequent enquiry. No action would be taken in respect of any officers.

Appeals following a murder conviction are fairly common although are not a foregone conclusion; they can be applied for only where there are procedural grounds to warrant one; an example being if a judge were to make a serious error when applying a point of law and therefore violating procedural rules. Forming the opinion that the jury simply got it wrong and wanting another shot at it is, unsurprisingly, not sufficient grounds. An appeal therefore will almost never be a re-assessment of the evidence already put forward and almost always based on a point of law not being applied properly.

Re-trials, however, are different and relatively rare, and would only be granted if significant new evidence were to come to light following a conviction, and that said evidence was not reasonably available at the time. It would not, for example, be grounds for a re-trial if the evidence had been available but simply overlooked. It could, however, be grounds if a critical piece of evidence was later proven to be falsified. Understandably, the threshold for allowing a retrial is incredibly high.

Following Jeremy's conviction, he was incarcerated in Wormwood Scrubs Prison, London and it was while he was here that his first appeal was lodged in November 1986. The basis of this claim was essentially that the summing up by Justice Drake was misleading and biased. It would take a couple of years, but in March 1988 this appeal was refused by a single judge, Mr Justice Caulfield, at the Court of Appeal. Following this it was submitted again and in 1989 was argued at a full court of appeal which consisted of Lord Chief Justice of England Lord Lane, Mr Justice Roch and Mr Justice Henry.

Jeremy's solicitor Rivlin argued again that the summing up had been unfair. He further elaborated that they felt Justice Drake had repeatedly and unfairly ridiculed Bamber's defence, that his handling of Julie's testimony was flawed and that his behaviour had generally been geared towards undermining the defence. As might be expected, this perceived criticism of a fellow Justice didn't go down well with the panel, and the appeal was again dismissed.

Jeremy is nothing if not persistent and following this he set about finding further evidence on which to appeal. Having been denied once he had now lost his right to legal aid and would henceforth be required to conduct his own research which he launched into with determination. Whether it is because he is truly innocent or because he has plenty of time on his hands is debatable, but he had by now been moved to Full

Sutton Prison, Yorkshire and it was from here that he worked on the case and trawled through the documents available to him.

As a by-product of his search for further evidence, by December 1990, Jeremy had discovered and listed twenty-six alleged grievances against Essex Police and submitted them to the Police Complaints Authority. As a result, the City of London Police investigated and responded to the claims, upholding not a single one of them. Jeremy was informed of this decision in August 1992 which resulted in him taking part in a dirty protest, smearing faeces on the walls of his cell which he said he was driven to out of 'sheer frustration.'[3] Amongst the allegations made were that the blood evidence in the silencer had been deliberately contaminated, and that witness statements had also been tampered with. However, the result of the investigation was that again, no disciplinary action would be taken against any member of Essex Police.

Jeremy was moved again and by 1991 was incarcerated at Gartree Prison, Leicestershire. While awaiting the results of his police grievances, he continued to work on finding sufficient grounds for a further appeal against his conviction and his next attempt came in 1993, the crux of it being that the blood evidence discovered in the silencer and determined to be Sheila's was flawed and that the possibility that it may have been a mixture of June and Nevill's blood could not be discounted. This alleged fresh evidence was discovered by independent forensic expert Mark Webster and formed part of the petition to be referred to the Court of Appeal in September of that year.

Essentially, Webster proposed that the silencer could have contained the blood of both June and Nevill Bamber. Supposing that one of the flakes of blood discovered and subsequently tested was an amalgam of their blood, Webster showed through experiments that if half the flake was tested and found to show enzyme AK1 and the other half was tested and found to show enzyme A then 'the result obtained will be indistinguishable from the result which would be obtained from a single source of blood group A (AK1).[34] In layman's terms, the blood which was determined to have come from Sheila alone could in theory have been made up from two halves of a flake made up of the mixed blood of June and Nevill. Of course, this doesn't prove that the silencer was not on the gun when Sheila was shot, but rather casts doubt on the certainty that the blood could *only* have belonged to Sheila. At great expense the team also hired Professor Herbert Leon MacDonald to reassess the evidence surrounding Sheila's death, but this appeared to backfire when he concluded that, in his opinion, Sheila had not committed suicide but like the rest of her family had been shot by someone else.

The Home Secretary refused the petition in July 1994. Jeremy's attempt to challenge this decision was then refused in April 1995 but his attempts at securing an appeal were not over; his case was inherited from the Home Office by the newly formed Criminal Cases Review Commission (CCRC) in March 1997. It would be four years later that they agreed there were grounds to refer the case to the Court of Appeal. Again, the blood evidence on the silencer was key, but this time supported by a further allegation by Jeremy's defence team that, using DNA from Sheila's biological mother for comparison, they had proven that the blood on the silencer could not have belonged to Sheila.

Subsequently the CCRC referred the case to the Court of Appeal in March 2001, securing a hearing in 2002 which took place on 17 October at the Royal Courts of Justice in London. Jeremy's defence was led by Michael Turner QC who was now representing him and alleged fourteen separate grounds for the conviction being unsafe. However, of these points, the issue of the DNA in the silencer was deemed most relevant, and it was on this which the judges presiding over the case focussed.

The defence asserted that not only did the blood not belong to Sheila, but that, by using statistical analysis of DNA from Pamela Boutflour, that it belonged to her sister, June. This assertion became less confident as more evidence was produced, however, and both the defence and prosecution admitted they 'could not exclude Sheila'[5] as being a contributor to the samples tested. Essentially the complexity of the mixed sample was such that no real conclusion could be drawn, only surmised. Mark Webster, whose evidence had formed part of the attempted appeal back in 1993 was called by the defence but further damaged their case by confirming that the DNA testing results were 'completely meaningless'[6] given the totality of the other evidence represented. It was not even confirmed that the sample tested consisted of blood. The appeal court upheld Jeremy's conviction.

The CCRC seem to have played a major part in Jeremy's attempts at appeals so far and potentially continue to do so, although at the time of writing, their website states that:

Jeremy Bamber was convicted in October 1986 of murder and received a sentence of life imprisonment. The CCRC inherited an application for review of the conviction from the Home Office in March 1997. At trial, the jury considered whether Mr Bamber had shot five members of his family, as argued by the prosecution, or whether Mr Bamber's sister, Sheila Caffell, might have shot the other four victims before shooting herself, as contended by the defence. The prosecution had told the court that a silencer had been used and that traces of blood on the silencer were found by the blood grouping tests then available to have been compatible with Ms Caffell but none of the other victims. It was part of the prosecution case that if the silencer was contaminated with Ms Caffell's blood when she was shot, it was impossible that she could also have been the person who pulled the trigger. During review, the CCRC obtained new expert DNA evidence indicating that the blood on the silencer could not have derived from Ms Caffell but could have come from one of the other victims. The CCRC considered that this evidence undermined the prosecution's argument as presented to the jury and to which the trial judge gave considerable emphasis in his summing up. The CCRC referred the conviction in March 2001. The Court of Appeal upheld the conviction in December 2002.[7]

However, they have certainly been involved since 2002, in fact in March 2004 Jeremy's legal team submitted another request to the CCRC on the basis that vital information had been withheld from them during their investigations. The CCRC declined immediately and again in March 2007. There was just not enough scope for an appeal, they concluded.

Ever determined, the team submitted yet again to the CCRC in 2010, based on three arguments; that undisclosed evidence might show that someone other than Sheila or Jeremy was guilty, that they had evidence that Sheila had murdered the others before committing suicide, and that either of these two arguments proved Jeremy's innocence. They now seemed to be moving away from the DNA and blood evidence in the silencer and rather focussing on the fact they believe Sheila was still alive in the house, referencing their belief that police had initially discovered one male and one female in the kitchen and that Sheila had initially been discovered unconscious in the kitchen and then fled upstairs and killed herself when the police arrived.

In February 2011 the CCRC said they were again, provisionally not going ahead with moving this forward to the Court of Appeal but welcomed him to resubmit within a year. This he did, with Simon McKay QC agreeing to represent him. The team came up with more alleged evidence to back their claims this time, with ballistics expert Phillip Boyce maintaining that the marks on Nevill's back were made by the barrel, and not the silencer, of the .22 rifle. Despite their confidence, a month later the CCRC confirmed they would not be referring Jeremy's case to the Court of Appeal, stating that 'matters of pure speculation or unsubstantiated allegation constitute neither new evidence nor new argument.'[8] Many may have given up by now, but not Jeremy. He and his team immediately instructed McKay to issue proceedings for a judicial review of the decision. The High Court refused it on 29 November 2012.

CAMPAIGN

She's got Hold of one of my Guns

This last refusal occurred, at the time of writing, thirteen years ago, and in the intervening years Jeremy and his campaign team have been busy building the case for perhaps their final attempt at appeal, but if several previous attempts have failed, on what basis are they now pursuing it once more? The short answer is, apparently, new evidence which has spawned a plethora of theories as to what allegedly happened on 7 August 1985. Following the release of previously unseen documents in 2011 Jeremy's team claim to, through evidence found within them, have discovered cast iron proof that Jeremy is innocent.

This is based mainly on said evidence proving not only that the silencer evidence is moot, but that Sheila was alive in the house during the siege. On the face of it, this sounds compelling. If it can be unequivocally established that Sheila was alive, then it logically follows that Jeremy is innocent. However, does the evidence categorically *prove* this, or has the information simply been interpreted in such a way that might suggest that Sheila was alive?

The Phone Call

One of the key contentions is the claim that Nevill Bamber himself called the police at 3.26 am on 7 August. If true, this of course explicitly corroborates Jeremy's version of events. This alleged proof is found within two separate call logs which Jeremy's team in turn claim reference two separate calls; one made by Nevill at 3.26 am followed by another by Jeremy at 3.36 am. Those who believe Jeremy to be guilty suggest that they both refer to the same phone call, as do the police officers who took the calls, and logged them.

Two separate call logs do indeed exist. One was recorded by 1990 (West's Badge Number) at 3.36 am. It details the 'sender' as Mr Bamber 9 Head Street, Goldhanger (Jeremy's address), and notes Jeremy's phone number as 88645. This suggests that 1990 (West) received a call from the sender, Jeremy Bamber. It reads:

> *'Father phoned (age 62)*
> *"Please come over your sister has gone crazy and has the gun"*
> *phone went dead.*
> *Father Mr Bamber aH/A White House Farm, Toleshunt [sic] D'Arcy Tel. Mald 860209*
> *Sister Sheila Bamber Age 27*
> *Has history of mental illness*
> *Action taken*
> *HQ/R informed*
> *CW informed and unit (??) despatched CA5 to scene*
> *a/insp? Informed*
> *Informant requested to attend scene*[1]

The other log was recorded by MB (6), or Malcolm Bonnett, at 3.26 am. This one details the sender as CD (1990), or Police Constable West at Chelmsford. As with the first log, it therefore seems clear that Bonnett was recording the details of a call he had received from the sender, Police Constable West. This one read:

> *'Daughter gone beserk.*
> *Mr Bamber*
> *White House Fm*
> *Tollshunt [sic] D'arcy*

Daughter Sheila Bamber, aged 26 yrs has got hold of one of my guns.

Message passed to CD by the son of Mr Bamber after the phone went dead. Mr Bamber has a collection of shotguns and .410s.'

Actions
CD contacting CW by landline. 3.56 GPO have checked phone line to farmhouse and confirm phone left off hook. CM 860209[2]

What makes it clear that Malcolm Bonnet was logging the content of the call he had received from West is that he records, following the content of the message itself; 'Message passed to CD by the son of Mr Bamber' at the end of his log, with CD being Chelmsford. Essentially, this second log seems to be Bonnett's transcript of what West was telling him that in turn, Jeremy had told him; that they both refer to one call made by Jeremy Bamber to West.

The obvious issue here is that Bonnett's call from West is recorded at 3.26 am, ten minutes *before* West records his call from Jeremy Bamber. If correct, of course it is impossible for West to have called Bonnett at 3.26 am and relayed the contents of a call which had not yet happened. It seems that this is at the crux of the theory that one of these calls was in fact placed by Nevill Bamber, coupled with the ambiguous way in which the message was transcribed and the fact that Sheila's age differs between the logs, suggesting that two separate people made them. Bonnett appears to have recorded word for word what West was telling him, that Sheila has 'got hold of one of *my* guns'. This has since been interpreted as a direct quote from Nevill either via West, or to Bonnett directly; it is often not clear which.

While it's easy to see why this disparity in the timings has sparked interest, it's rather difficult to pin down the specifics of the many theories which now surround it, for example who exactly did Nevill allegedly speak to? The most logical interpretation of this evidence would be that if the 3.26 am call was made by Nevill, as the team suggest, then it was Bonnett who spoke to him. This is certainly one which is widely put forward by many who believe that the call log evidence proves Jeremy's innocence. It is the one which appears in the documentary *The Bambers; Murder at the Farm* in which West addresses this and the call time discrepancy and which he later addressed during a podcast interview:

'[the first log] is the log of my phone call that I received from Jeremy, timed 03.36.

I'm the receiver 1990 - that was my Collar number. I've written - Father phoned Age 62 - "Please come over, your sister has gone crazy and has the gun" - phone went dead.

So, if you then look at the log that Malcolm Bonnett, MB (6) started... the sender he's recorded as CD, in brackets 1990. So, the person who spoke to Malcolm Bonnett is myself. So, all of the information on there refers to what I have said to Malcolm Bonnett. He's receiving it third hand and has transposed it third hand. Malcolm Bonnett recorded the time that I spoke to him at 03.26. Much is made that this referred to a phone call that Nevill Bamber made, but nowhere on there does that say Nevill Bamber, and of course if I'd rung Malcolm Bonnett ten minutes after he'd had a phone call from Nevill Bamber, you tend to think the first words out of his mouth would be - "That's a coincidence, Mick... I've just had a phone call from Nevill Bamber" - Nothing of the sort.

There was an error over the time... I looked at a clock. There was no time stamp on a computer that there would be today. Some of the errors were just human nature. It's risible in my opinion to think that at any stage I was part of a conspiracy. I was a young police officer, but that's all it was... a simple error made by a young police constable at half past three in an uneventful, up until then, night shift.'[3]

So, the explanation for this, and indeed the one which was addressed at trial, is that West made a mistake when glancing at the clock and recorded the time of his call from Jeremy as 3.36 am rather than 3.26 am, the actual time of his call to Malcolm Bonnett.

However, the official line on Jeremy's campaign website is that both calls were taken by West, one from Nevill at 3.26 am followed by another from Jeremy at 3.36 am; that West spoke to Nevill, called Bonnett to relay the information, ended that call and then took a second call from Jeremy and then called Bonnett again, who subsequently added the 'message passed to CD by the son of Mr Bamber' following this second call, neatly explaining this entry away.

Does the ambiguous wording and error in the timestamp make this worth a second look? Possibly, yes. Is this cast iron proof that Nevill Bamber called the police himself that night? Almost certainly, no, because the fact remains that neither West or Bonnett, either at the time of the investigation or since, have ever suggested that they took a phone call from Nevill Bamber on 7 August.

Sheila was alive

This is a very definite and bold statement to make, and yet Jeremy's team do make it, regularly. Broken down, the assertion that Sheila was alive inside the farmhouse is based on several different pieces of information, beginning with a question as simple as whether the phone in the kitchen at White House Farm was off the hook or engaged following Nevill's alleged call to Jeremy. What difference might this make? Jeremy stated in an interview that following the call from his father he tried to call him back, but that 'it was engaged, so Dad was ringing someone else,'[4] further adding to the theory that Nevill was at that point on the phone to the police. This also suggests that the status of the phone line changed throughout the night, implying that someone inside the house was sporadically lifting and replacing the receiver and possibly making phone calls.

However, the use of language to describe the state of the phone lines to imply they were constantly changing can be misleading. To a person trying to get through on the phone, there is simply no difference between the sound they would hear if the phone was engaged, or if it were off the hook. The result of someone either already being on a call or having taken the phone off the hook is the same, a busy signal. Jeremy's team assert that 'a telephone being off the hook and engaged are two completely separate and unique states of the telephone line which emit distinctively differing audible tones when the number is dialled.'[5] This is dismissed by the retired British Telecom engineer who was interviewed for this section as 'Rubbish. There is only one engaged tone, and that occurs when the phone is off the hook, or when someone is in conversation.'[6]

What's different of course, is when British Telecom become involved and are able to confirm the *actual* status of the phone line. When Jean Rowe checked the line that evening and found it to be 'off the hook' she would have been able to listen in and hear if anything was going on in the room. Similarly, if she checked the line and found it to be engaged, she would have been able to listen to whatever conversation might have been taking place. *She* was able to tell the difference between these two states, but someone trying to call the house would not. When she began to listen in, she could hear the dog barking, meaning the phone was most definitely off the hook. That's not to say someone hadn't been using the phone earlier before she checked in of course, but the fact remains that Jeremy cannot say with certainty that his father was on another call when he tried to ring him back. He might have been, but it can't be proven one way or another by the tone Jeremy heard.

However, when the police finally gained entry into the farm later that evening, the classic rotary phone from which the call was made was found with the handset off and placed next to it. This seems to corroborate Jeremy's story that someone had put their finger on the receiver to terminate the call rather than replace the receiver, the implication being that an aggressor, i.e. Sheila, abruptly terminated it rather than Nevill calmly replacing the receiver. Of course, this is a moot point if Jeremy is guilty as he presumably would have simply staged this scene by leaving the phone off the hook himself.

The most compelling theory regarding the use of the phones that night, if proven to be true, is the claim that someone from within the farmhouse made a 999 call at 6.09 am on 7 August, while Jeremy was standing outside surrounded by several police officers. This would appear to prove Jeremy's innocence once and for all and yet this compelling, allegedly cast-iron fact appears to stem from just one entry in the scene log after Malcolm Bonnett recorded that at 5.25 am the 'firearms team are in conversation with a person from inside the farm' followed by another recording at 5.29 am recording a 'challenge to persons inside the house met with no response.'[7]

Firstly, it appears the police were trying, and failing, to establish whether anyone, and in particular Sheila, was still alive inside the farmhouse. While Jeremy's campaign team suggest that the 'conversation with a person from inside the farm' referred to Sheila, further cementing an alibi for Jeremy, this appears to be the only reference to it and is generally interpreted as a conversation with Jeremy, given the distinction between talking to someone 'inside the farm' and 'inside the house.' Again, not a single officer who attended the scene that evening has ever reported hearing a voice from within the farmhouse, let alone a full two-way conversation with Sheila. The phrase 'in conversation with a person from inside the farm' is, however, if not conclusive then at least ambiguous and open to interpretation.

Following this and in terms of the alleged phone call itself, the entry in the log which points to it having been made is an instruction to the operator to 'open 999 line set up (direct link to house with phone off hook)' at 6.09 am. It was followed at 7.47 am with the instruction to 'close down '999' open line' with the 'operator notified'[8] at 7.48 am, after the bodies had been discovered, implying the line had been taken over for around one hour and forty minutes while the subsequent raid took place. This opening of the line appears to be the result of Adams's instruction to Jean Rowe to link the line directly to Essex Police Headquarters to allow them to continue to monitor it but has since been interpreted by those who believe Jeremy to be innocent as a direct 999 call made by somebody in the house, presumed to be Sheila.

Further proof, they say, is that this call immediately triggered the arrival of two ambulances which arrived at around 6.30 am although these had allegedly already been requested by Bews with the instructions that one was 'for immediate use and one for standby' in anticipation of what they might find when they eventually gained entry. While this leap might seem tenuous at best, an article by Heidi Blake, published in the New Yorker in July 2024 goes one step further in having tracked down and interviewed the police officer who allegedly took the call, Nicholas Milbank, whose statement at the time made no mention of a 999 call being received but that he had simply been asked to monitor the line and had heard nothing until the officers entered the premises. The article alleges however that this statement was fabricated as it 'had not been signed; Milbank's name had been typed on the signature line'[9] apparently corroborated by the officer himself who has no recollection of the statement being taken.

In his interview with Blake, Milbank agreed that 'from what I can remember, someone phoned 999' from 'inside the farmhouse'. He went on to say he had not been spoken to but 'recalled hearing what might have been muffled speech—perhaps a "voice or a radio"—and noises that could have been "a door opening and closing, or a chair being moved".' When Blake asked if this suggested that someone had been alive in the house, "Well, obviously," Milbank replied'[10]

One dead male and one dead female

The 999 call theory is just one example which Jeremy's team say proves that Sheila was alive in the house, with another being they are adamant that Sheila was lying unconscious in the kitchen when the police first broke in. Again, if true, this is compelling, however they postulate one scenario which can charitably be described as a far-fetched, in which Collins was correct when he identified the first body he saw on approaching the kitchen as female; it was in fact Sheila. Therefore, there must initially have been two bodies located in the kitchen on arrival, one female, Sheila, and one male, Nevill. Their explanation as to how Sheila was later found dead upstairs; she was simply unconscious following the first, non-fatal attempt at her own life, and when the police arrived, she 'came to' and ran upstairs where she successfully shot and killed herself.

It's worth noting that again, this is not corroborated by any of the officers who entered the building that morning, in the same way that Bonnett and West categorically denied speaking to Nevill Bamber on the phone. The source of the theory is again one sentence recorded on the scene log and which stated 'one dead male and one dead female in kitchen' recorded at 7.37 am and it remains the single reference to a female body *in the kitchen.* The corresponding communication log at 7.38 am records the discovery of 'one dead male and one dead female found on entry to premises' along with yet another concurrent log at 8.10 am which stated a 'further three bodies found. Five dead in total.'[11]

According to his statement, Collins entered the premises, established that Nevill was dead, searched the ground floor then arrived at the stairs where, in his mirror, he saw the body of who he later learned to be June. One could argue that an alternative scenario is that the 'one male and one female' might refer to Nevill and then June Bamber, with the further three later discovered being Sheila, Nicholas and Daniel. The reference to a body of each gender being discovered in the kitchen could be explained by Collins's initial mistake in thinking that Nevill was female, with this being recorded in the log.

Retired Police Sergeant Andy Bone confirms that the latter is a much more likely scenario. Perhaps what some people fail to realise or prefer to ignore, is that as events are happening in quick succession it is an officer's duty to record each one in the moment and under no circumstances would they go back later and correct what was recorded if it was subsequently found to be written in error. Therefore, it seems reasonable that on initially hearing that a female had been found in the kitchen, this is exactly what was recorded in the log, along with the male, Nevill, despite them being one and the same person. It certainly seems far more realistic a set of circumstances than Sheila reviving and running upstairs to shoot herself which was again not witnessed by any of the several officers who were by then located within the farmhouse itself.

Bone recalls a story during his time as a serving officer which neatly sums up this kind of incident:

In about 2001 I was on duty on nights, and we get a report over the radio of 40 people fighting with baseball bats. The location given made this more than plausible. We deploy, calling up for further resources on route. On arrival it turns out there were 4 people fighting wearing baseball caps.

Somewhere in the log will be the record of 40 people and baseball bats. A simple mistake that happens all the time.[12]

So, while his is a somewhat humorous anecdote, a similar mistake made during a raid of a potential murder scene can have far more serious outreaching consequences. As a result of it, Jeremy's team assert that the two initial bodies found were Sheila and Nevill, and the further three were June and the boys. However, this doesn't appear to make sense if, as they say, Sheila was initially downstairs and then later appeared upstairs; surely then, they would have reported finding another *four* bodies. Unless they found June, Daniel and Nicholas and, while processing this discovery, Sheila nipped in behind them and shot herself without anyone seeing or hearing her do so. Not only that, but surely, they would have wondered where on earth the female body that they discovered downstairs had now disappeared to when they re-entered the kitchen later.

To back up claims that Sheila was still alive when the police entered the farmhouse, Jeremy's team say that the noise made by Rozga while covering the office upstairs and subsequently heard by Hall from the kitchen was not Rozga, but Sheila, perhaps derived from Hall's testimony that he was 'calling to Sheila Bamber to make herself known'[13] before realising that the noise had been made by his colleague. However, they may potentially have got the two separate staircases mixed up in this scenario as they state that there were 'no police upstairs' when Hall heard the noise which they say was made by Sheila running upstairs to the bedroom, presumably to shoot herself. They are correct, there were no police upstairs in the bedrooms at that point, because Hall heard the noise from the stairs leading from the scullery, not the main staircase. Hall was in the kitchen, not the hallway. They assert that 'there was no one upstairs at that time, Rozga went up later'[14] but don't appear to have any evidence to support this and it directly contradicts the witness statements from the raid team.

Not only are Jeremy's supporters adamant that Sheila was in the kitchen at the time of the raid team's arrival, but also that she had been seen moving around within the farmhouse numerous times during the run up to entry. Firstly, of course this was due to Bews's initial impression that he had seen movement in one of the windows upstairs and despite not corroborating this at the time, Jeremy went on later to substantiate this with a claim that the lights were on in his parent's bedroom, then Myall saw someone standing in the bedroom door. Bews, he says, agreed and that this person then moved again, leaving them all in no doubt about what they had seen, claiming that 'all three of us confirmed we had seen an adult.' However, he does admit that 'I've recalled snippets of info from my memory that happened. PC Bews said that he thought the person he had seen had something in their hands, PC Myall hadn't noticed that and nor had I.' He goes on to say that 'I'm pretty certain we'd seen someone walk towards the window in the master bedroom' and that 'someone pulled the curtains closed.'[15] Again, this is not corroborated by Bews or Myall and is the result of a recollection by Jeremy written some thirty years after the event, to a journalist sympathetic to his cause who was writing a book about his innocence.

Myall's recollection is that on arrival the lights were on in the kitchen with the curtains open, and that the lights were on behind drawn curtains in the bathroom and the twins' bedroom. Collins later agreed, saying that he saw the following lights were switched on; 'kitchen with no curtains at window' and 'two upstairs rooms directly above the window; one with pink curtains closed and one with blue curtains closed. There was only one other light switched on in the house which was situated directly over the main door.' He went on to confirm that all doors and windows were closed apart from that 'the master bedroom window was pulled down about three inches.'[16]

It seems that the one piece of what could be perceived as evidence of someone opening and closing curtains and turning lights on and off, is a statement by Police Constable Alan Brown whereby he recorded that 'I could see that the upstairs window in my concern was slightly open at the top and the curtains were closed' but that crime scene photographs show the master bedroom curtains were open.'[17] Therefore, what appears to be the interpretation of one inconsistency which might at best warrant a second look at which curtains were open, has morphed into a scenario in which an intruder was clearly seen moving around inside the house, opening and shutting curtains and turning lights on and off with regularity. There is no contemporary record on any of the logs that any alleged movement was seen by anyone other than Bews and indeed even his encounter was not logged at the time but recounted at a later date. There is no record of Jeremy having commented on seeing any movement within the house during the time he was outside with the officers.

Brown is however involved in another sighting involving Jeapes who had taken over from Alexander-Smart covering the kitchen and front door area outside (described in her statement as white/red) when the latter joined the raid team, and she stated that 'I could also see a window on the first floor of white/red side where the building is clad in grey brick in which was what appeared to be a rifle leaning against the window.' She follows this with 'there was no sign of movement in the house.'[18] Jeremy's team say that the bedroom to which she refers is the small bedroom next to the master bedroom. There is no reference to this rifle being found inside the house and no photographic evidence of it, but it is claimed that it is without doubt the .22 rifle later found on Sheila's body and, therefore, proof she was alive inside the house, moving it around until she finally shot herself with it.

The counter argument is that what they thought was a rifle was something else, or that they were mistaken. If true though, this suggests that Sheila was still alive at around 7.10am when it was spotted and, because it was not mentioned in any report or photographed at all, that 'therefore Sheila had to have moved the rifle from the window between the time of these sightings and 07.35 when the police broke in.'[19] This, however, seems to contradict their earlier assertion that Sheila was lying unconscious on the floor of the kitchen when the raid team entered at just after 7.30 am leaving her really rather a narrow window of opportunity to do everything the team suggest took place. One might also question why she had started to 'go berserk' at 3.00 am and kill her entire family but decided to leave it until the raid team entered before turning the gun on herself.

Corruption

The problem with each of these allegations is that they are not corroborated contemporaneously; nobody admitted to speaking to Nevill or Sheila on the night, there's no record in any of the logs or statements of Sheila being seen in the kitchen and no real solid reference to recognisable movement taking place inside the house. This seems to be explained away, however, under the convenient narrative of police corruption.

Essex Police have always been under suspicion by Jeremy's team of either destroying or withholding evidence, and to buy into this theory, one would have to believe that the many dozens of officers attending White House Farm on 7 August were complicit in hiding any evidence which pointed towards Sheila being the culprit and focussing unfairly on or falsifying evidence which pointed towards Jeremy. This does beg the overarching question; why? If the initial reaction from everyone involved was that Sheila had committed a murder-suicide, what was it that suddenly motivated the Essex Police Force in its entirety to not only about turn but to actually invent evidence to put an innocent man behind bars? It wasn't as if they were under any pressure to turn in a result given that they were presented with a perfectly reasonable explanation of murder-suicide which they could have gone with right from the start.

What would Bonnett or West's motive be to maintain a lie for nearly forty years and pretend they had never taken a call from Nevill Bamber that night? Why would Collins, during the adrenaline fuelled seconds as he entered the farm think to himself 'I've just seen Sheila's body on the floor, but I won't mention it just yet in case we plan on framing the brother later?' Why has the officer who was reportedly 'in conversation with' Sheila in the early hours never disclosed what was said, surely a crucial piece of information, or even acknowledged that the conversation took place?

The issue with accusations of corruption is that they never end with just one or two people being involved and in this case the theory has spiralled to include Essex Police, Jeremy's family and even the judge who presided over the trial. Furthermore, if the theories are to be believed then the family are at the root of it all; they quite simply decided that they didn't want Jeremy to inherit their fortune and to keep it in the family they were then able to exert enough influence over Essex Police to change the course of the whole investigation to benefit themselves. This influence then became so strong that several police officers were willing to put their livelihoods and reputations on the line so that Jeremy Bamber, a man who up until then the majority of them had never met, could be robbed of his inheritance.

Indeed, it *was* Ann and David who helped to drive the investigation in a different direction, having first been alerted by Jeremy's manner following the murders and then almost taking on the role of amateur detectives in trying to track down the real killer. However, it's as likely that they were keen to facilitate Jeremy's arrest because they believed him to be a cold-blooded killer as it is that their motivation was to make sure he was disinherited because they thought of him as the 'cuckoo' in the nest. One might argue that far from their actions being duplicitous, they would have been foolish *not* to pursue the idea that Jeremy might be responsible.

The issue with accusing the police of lying or falsifying evidence is that reliance then on any of the said evidence holds much less weight; essentially it suggests that they must be lying when their evidence is inconvenient yet telling the truth when it is supportive of a theory; the campaign team will often refer to the fact that their proof comes not from speculation but rather from documentation and police logs, written by the very people they accuse of lying. Another example might be a phrase from Collins's statement in which he described the body of Sheila and that what appeared to be blood 'had run' down her neck. This is often cited as proof that Sheila had not long been dead, and therefore used to bolster the idea that she shot herself after the raid team had entered. However, blood which 'had run' rather than blood which 'was running' down her neck can mean two very different things and is often misquoted as such but still, is an example of perhaps what might be described as cherry picking of evidence.

The Silencer

The crux of this evidence of police corruption is the assertion that the silencer, arguably the most pivotal in Jeremy's conviction alongside Julie Mugford's testimony, should never have been admitted into evidence because not one but two, if not more silencers were found in White House Farm during the investigation, seriously calling into question its validity. Firstly, of course, there is the implication that the family simply planted it in order to shore up the case against Jeremy. Furthermore, in a video on Jeremy's supporter site explaining how they conclude that the silencer evidence is moot, they state that: 'you will be able to see how the evidence presented at trial was not from one exhibit, but from as many as five moderators. Collected and examined at different times, the exhibit evidence was effectively stitched together to form what was the cornerstone of the fabricated prosecution case against an innocent man. We know for sure that the moderator never played a part in the tragedies that unfolded at White House Farm.'[20]

This six-minute-long video explains how the original evidence suggested that firstly the moderator contained traces of red paint from the AGA in the kitchen, implying a fight with Nevill Bamber. However, the paint, they say, was not actually found on the silencer used in court and in fact had been falsified, due to the fact they could not see any evidence of red paint flakes on the floor beneath the AGA in the crime scene photographs, implying this scratch had been made later to justify the evidence.

Although the family handed in one sound moderator to the police, police files suggest that another moderator was already undergoing fingerprint analysis a couple of days previously, and that a newspaper article stated that 'at an early stage of the investigation a silencer was taken away from White House Farm for forensic examination.'[21] Given the press's justified reputation for getting things wrong, this could have referred to the one found by the family, however following this the video stated that a silencer belonging to David was handed in to police in September 1985 followed by one belonging to Robert in October of the same year.

The relevance of this is that Jeremy's campaign team allege that the forensic examinations which the police say were carried out on the single moderator used at trial were in fact carried out on three different moderators, given that the first was labelled 'item 22' with reference SC/688/85 with the next being labelled 'item 23' with reference SC/786/85 and the third reverting back to 'item 22' but retaining the new case number which, they say, was allocated due to Jeremy now being a suspect, while the first had been labelled prior to this. During these investigations, they assert that the position of the paint flakes changed, meaning that they must have been testing different moderators. Although evidence of two moderators doesn't necessarily mean the evidence found in one of them is not still valid, in answer to the suggestion that some of the theories of Jeremy's innocence are based on speculation, Philip Walker from Jeremy's campaign team explains that this is at least one piece which is based not on interpretation but fact:

> *'The fact that police, and forensic records record two [moderators], with two different forensic tags, different item numbers, different physical characteristics, different contaminants on each, that the City of London Police enquiry in 1991 concluded there were two, the police announced at a packed press conference that they had found one on the day (in addition to the one that all parties accept was found by the relatives three days later), and many other pieces of evidence pointing to two, is not a matter of opinion. It is an empirical assessment of the facts from the official documentation and public records. Of course, we will find out shortly, whether our conclusion is shared by the judiciary.'*[22]

He is talking of the very latest attempt at appeal. Following the failed attempt in 2012 Jeremy and his campaign team have focussed on providing proof that Sheila was alive in the house on the night of the murders and so by March 2021, yet another submission was made to the CCRC.

This submission consisted originally of eight separate points which are listed on Jeremy Bamber's official campaign website as:

Issue 1 - The silencers – The corpus of evidence that two silencers featured in the case and were forensically examined. There are multiple grounds regarding chain of evidence and contaminate issues.

Why is this important? One example of the many grounds here is on the Crown's assertions that a tiny flake of blood inside one of the silencers was a match for Sheila Caffell only. The jury were not told it was also an exact match for the beneficiary Robert Boutflour. This links to Issue 6 and Issue 8.

Issue 2 – The telephone calls – Substantial fresh evidence regarding the telephone call from Nevill Bamber to Jeremy and two phone calls to the police, one made by Nevill at 03:26, one made by Jeremy at 03:36.

Why this is important? This is Jeremy's alibi. The Crown told the jury that a single phone call was made from Jeremy to the police. Proving that Jeremy and the police had a call from Nevill Bamber to alert them to the unfolding incident is Jeremy's alibi.

Issue 3 – The integrity of the scene – Detailed grounds including fresh evidence regarding the police interference with the scene and the exhibits.

Why this is important? Movement of items and the deceased by the police prior and during crime scene photographs being taken which contradicted evidence in disclosed police statements. An untruthful and inaccurate scenario was then created by the police at a later stage in an attempt to implicate Jeremy Bamber.

Issue 4 – The windows at White House Farm - Multiple grounds in relation to the kitchen and the downstairs shower room windows that undermines the Crown's evidence at trial.

Why this is important? The windows were supposedly Jeremy Bamber's means of entry and exit to the locked house. The fresh evidence proves there was no signs of forced entry and therefore, no one entered the house.

Issue 5 – Sheila Caffell – Multiple grounds which prove Sheila was alive until after the raid team entered the house. In addition, fresh evidence regarding Sheila at the scene.

Why this is important? Jeremy Bamber was standing outside the house in the company of many police officers when activity was logged as occurring within the house. Therefore, he cannot have been involved.

*Issue 6 - **Photographic issues*** – Multiple, very focused grounds regarding the non-disclosure of case photographs in respect of many individual case issues.

Why this is important? One example is that Essex Police and scientists took lots of photographs of the case silencers which have never been disclosed. These would prove two featured in the case but were merged into one exhibit which the crown claimed was on the gun and had blood inside from Sheila Caffell. This links to Issue 1.

*Issue 7 - **Complaints against police officers*** – Detailed and focused on the actions of two key police officers and their interference in the case from 1985 to date.

Why this is important? The senior Scenes of Crime officer, DI Cook, and the Senior Investigating Officer, DSI Ainsley, retained undisclosed case material and exhibits they later supplied to members of the public. They were responsible for a range of actions in manipulating the case including lying to the Director of Public Prosecutions.

*Issue 8 - **Inheritance issues*** – Multiple grounds regarding the actions of the beneficiaries in the case and how the jury were deceived.

Why this is important? The wealth of evidence shows that there was clear motive for witnesses, including Jeremy Bamber's Uncle, Robert Boutflour to lie on oath [sic] in order to achieve the conviction.

This was the only way they would inherit from June's, Nevill's and Sheila's estates. This was undisclosed to the court when the jury asked if they had motive. This links to issue 1.[24]

One could argue that only someone who is truly innocent would continue to campaign so relentlessly. The counter argument is that Jeremy Bamber is a narcissistic psychopath, but his campaign team are convinced that the former is true, as one of them confidently claims on the back of this submission that 'we don't have any holes in our case. It cannot be refused this time.'[25]

The CCRC would appear to disagree. On 4 July 2025 they announced that they would not be referring Jeremy's case to appeal, at least not based on the four points on which they have reached a decision; the second silencer, Nevill's alleged phone call, the compromised integrity of the crime scene and the alleged 999 call. In their provisional statement of reasons, they state that the issues 'did not reach the threshold for a referral to the court of appeal'.[26]

Perhaps most damaging to the campaign is the dismissal of the 999-call theory, with the revelation that following the release of the New Yorker article Milbank 'subsequently provided a statement, saying "I have never to my knowledge spoken to the New Yorker," and that he did not know he had been talking to a journalist.'[27] The New Yorker refute this claim, but the former police officer has since sadly passed away, so further argument may prove futile.

The CCRC will continue to review the remaining six points but given that they have already dismissed the ones which arguably held the most promise for the campaign and despite the team's assurance that they will appeal the decision, it seems that the elusive chance of a retrial may finally have slipped through the net and got away for good.

The Tragedies

It is a common if not automatic reaction, to immediately appeal against a murder conviction and an understandable course of action under any circumstances other than that in which the perpetrator has confessed and accepts their fate; extreme examples being Jeffery Dahmer or Edmund Kemper, both serial killers from the United States who were positively verbose in their subsequent confessions and agreed that being behind bars was the safest place for both themselves and society at large.

Most however will immediately turn to appeal if they are able, and while it is unusual for this to be successful straight away, some long-term campaigns can and of course do, work. Take for example Barry George, convicted of killing British television presenter Jill Dando in 2001, coincidentally decided also by a jury with a majority of ten to one, rather than unanimous decision.

In a case which in some ways mirrors Jeremy's, several observers at the time considered the conviction to be unsafe, but Barry George's initial appeal was dismissed by the Court of Appeal. In 2006 however, new evidence was put forward by his team; that George was not capable of committing the crimes due to his mental disabilities. They also brought forward two new eye-witnesses pertaining to the nature of his arrest where guns were present. For George's campaign their complaint was against the Metropolitan rather than Essex Police but still involved allegations against the police of trying to falsify evidence in order to gain a conviction.

Finally, they presented the all-important firearms discharge residue (FDR) evidence which eventually led to his release 'which called into question the FDR evidence given at trial, as well as the significance apparently attached to that evidence.'[1] In 2007 the CCRC agreed to refer his case to the court of appeal, where in November of that year, Barry George's conviction was quashed. Following a retrial which was unable to present any scientific proof putting George at the crime scene and in fact eye-witnesses who put him somewhere else at the time of the murder, he was eventually acquitted on 1 August 2008.

George's sister, Michelle Bates, who campaigned on behalf of her brother is perhaps unsurprisingly listed as a patron of Jeremy's campaign team, as is Michael O'Brien, who, according to their website, 'was wrongly convicted of murdering a Cardiff Newsagent in 1988 and served 11 years in prison, 7 of those were with Jeremy Bamber.'[2] It's also not surprising that the team reference several successful appeals such as that of Andrew Malkinson who was convicted of rape in 2004 and served sixteen years in prison before being released for good behaviour. Following this however, he continued to appeal, and his conviction was finally quashed in 2023 on the basis of re-examined DNA samples.

One would be hard pushed to find a team of people willing to give up a considerable amount of their free time to campaign for the freedom of someone like, for example, the aforementioned Dahmer or Kemper. It does happen of course, for example the phenomenon of Hybristophilia (a sexual interest in and attraction to those who commit crimes) played no small part in the case of American serial killer Ted Bundy where his 'fans' dyed their hair in order to resemble his preferred victim's appearance and attended his court case in the hope of catching a glimpse of, or better still, talking to him. However, it's hard to believe that many of them would actually go so far as to campaign for his release although he did go on to marry one of his staunch supporters during his trial for murder in which he represented himself and was eventually convicted.

Not everyone convicted of murder can be the victim of a miscarriage of justice but the very fact that miscarriages do happen at all must leave an element of doubt in almost every case apart from those with clear cut irrefutable evidence, eyewitnesses to the crime itself and perhaps a confession. This is perfectly summed up by Dr Eady, another of Jeremy's supporters, who quoted Blackstone's law during an interview with the author; that 'it is better that ten guilty persons escape than that one innocent suffer'[3] which seems to succinctly sum up our motivation as human beings to seek justice.

However, it could be argued that in recent years the immediate knee-jerk reaction by armchair detectives that every high-profile conviction they see is unsafe has become increasingly common and arguably by those who are more and more detached, both physically and emotionally, from the person they are campaigning for. Historically, and in the pre-digital age, campaigns might be started up by the family and close friends of the convicted murderer. Now, millions of people across the globe are able to not only form an opinion of the veracity of a murder conviction but also, to some extent, feel that they are taking part in the actual investigation by trawling through 'evidence' often erroneously presented as fact online by random strangers. Not only that, but this 'evidence' will form the sole basis of their desire for justice rather than any real connection to the person they are defending. These 'campaigns' are often more about proving to themselves that they are able to solve a rather tricky puzzle or to catch out the nasty, corrupt establishment rather than any deep personal connection with the crime or its alleged perpetrator.

Two current examples might be the cases of Lucy Letby and Richard Allen. Lucy Letby is a nurse who was convicted in August 2023 of murdering eight babies in her care in the hospital in the United Kingdom where she worked; there are currently around twelve thousand people on the online message forum Reddit discussing whether or not she should have been found guilty. A further ninety-eight thousand are asking the same question about Richard Allen, who was found guilty of murdering teenagers Liberty German and Abby

Williams in November 2024 in the state of Delphi in America. Since then, there has been an outcry of people all over the world claiming they *know* they are innocent and calling for immediate appeals. This might seem to be on some level virtuous, but it is apparent that with this overwhelming desire to appeal, what the families of the victims might feel about this arguably crass outpouring of solidarity for the people who have been convicted of killing their loved ones is totally forgotten. One imagines that if the murders at White House Farm had occurred in the days of Reddit, then a very similar situation would have occurred but notwithstanding the lack of social media at the time, Jeremy boasts not only an increasingly large following of supporters online but also a real campaign team, which is much more unusual; his core supporters don't just argue about it online, they actually do something.

The Jeremy Bamber Innocence Campaign (JBIC) make some bold promises on their website and various social media channels; they are nothing if not confident. Their website states that they can 'prove unequivocally and once and for all that [Jeremy] was not responsible for the deaths of his family in 1985'[4] and theirs is a site jam-packed with information, or misinformation, depending on the reader's viewpoint. It is thorough but anything but balanced. JBIC are the team behind the recent CCRC submission in 2021 and according to the site, this is the trading name for Jeremy Bamber Campaign Ltd which was incorporated on 23 November 2015 by founding directors Trudi and Patrick Benjamin. Since then, Emma Morris, Yvonne Hartley, Lorna Lake and Philip Walker have been made directors, with Trudi and Patrick stepping down from their director roles in May 2020. Philip and Yvonne, and sometimes Emma, make the most prolific appearances on their YouTube channel and their *Jeremy Bamber and White House Farm Podcast.*

Aside from the directors the campaign team 'is made up of academics, lawyers, journalists, actors and producers, as well as business professionals. Some of us have known and worked with Jeremy on his case for many years.'[5] Perhaps in contrast to the majority of web sleuths trawling through evidence on the Letby and Allen cases, this team have at least met the person they are campaigning for. In one interview, Philip describes Jeremy as 'good company' with a 'good sense of humour' and Yvonne explains how thoughtful and caring he is, always thinking of others and that he's 'very supportive of us and the work we do to get the evidence of his innocence out.' He's resilient and 'bounces back and back and back from all these pushbacks and rejections.' Philip laments that 'he is just a normal person to whom a terrible misfortune has befallen.'[6]

No matter what the motivation behind it, their dedication and apparently genuine affection for Jeremy is undisputed. Yvonne said of him that 'the thing that keeps him going is that he knows he is innocent. We can surmise [and we] believe he is innocent, but he *knows* and that's what gives him the inner strength to cope with what has been a terrible ordeal.' She also goes on to describe how devastated she and the team were at the result of the judicial review which did not go their way; she was 'in floods of tears.' But Jeremy's response was 'it's fine. We get up, we move on' as 'he is absolutely determined, as we are, to prove that he's innocent.'[7]

Where does this dedication of the team stem from? It is obviously a complex issue, but it seems to be predominately a fight against what they perceive as a corrupt system, believing that Jeremy is a political prisoner because of his whole life tariff. They seem to be genuinely of the opinion that Jeremy was convicted due to the incompetence of the Essex Police Force who through a series of glaring errors found themselves having to cover their tracks, using Jeremy as the scapegoat; essentially, they say, the spiralling incompetence went too far, and it would now be far too embarrassing to admit their mistakes and let Jeremy out of prison. If Jeremy were really guilty, they say, he would have taken the chance of a deal at trial and might have been released by now, and so in his dedicated and continued protestation of his innocence he has proven himself.

They do have their own personal reasons for joining the campaign, with Yvonne revealing that her 'burning issue is the scratch marks', referring to the allegation that scratch marks found on the AGA to match paint samples found on the silencer were staged by police to bolster the silencer evidence. Yvonne became the forensic liaison manager on the team following her writing to Jeremy to give him her support. It's the 'best job in the world! Especially when you find evidence like yesterday!'[8] she says, although without elaborating on what that evidence was.

Philip's journey started when he read *Blood Relations – The definitive account of Jeremy Bamber and the White House Murders* by Roger Wilkes and came to the conclusion that there 'something a bit dodgy' about the case. He followed this years later having read *The Murders at White House Farm* by Carol Ann Lee, the '"in quotes" definitive account of the case'[9] with which he clearly did not agree. Philip runs the communication side of things for the team, however he later seemed reticent to talk to the author about his personal motivations; 'I appreciate your interest in my feelings about the case but, to be honest, until the case is settled, they don't really matter one way or the other. All that counts is the courts' views of the new evidence, which we hope to find out soon.'[10]

The campaign team's ultimate aim is, of course, Jeremy's exoneration and whilst their latest CCRC appeal has since been partially denied, the means by which they can continue to achieve this are mainly twofold. Firstly, they continue to campaign for the release of millions of pieces of information; a request which they say has been continually ignored by the police. They maintain that these documents hold the key to proving Jeremy's innocence and therefore a more successful CCRC application although this does seem to beg the question that if their case already contains no holes, what more do they need? Yvonne herself at one point explains that they 'don't need it',[11] but still want it to help shore up the defence they already have when the inevitable retrial occurs, something which is looking increasingly less likely.

Secondly, they need to keep the profile of the case in the public eye, and their method in doing so seems to be to attack the Essex Police, Julie Mugford, and the Boutflour and Pargeter families and because of this their campaign could be perceived as a very negative, rather than a positive one. It seeks to prove Sheila's guilt, the family's greed and the Essex Police's ineptitude or corruption far more often than it attempts to seek Jeremy's innocence. This element seems to mostly consist of the insistence that he is kind and supportive, helps fellow prisoners to read and write so that they can fight their own cases, is calm, never causes trouble and is a model prisoner. And he says he didn't do it, and they believe him.

When the campaign team talk about this case during their numerous podcast and video appearances, there is a running theme which isn't necessarily obvious at first, but which becomes more apparent with time. Rarely, if ever, do the campaign team refer to what happened in the early hours of 7 August 1985 as murder. Instead, they consistently and deliberately refer to the murders of June, Nevill, Sheila, Daniel and Nicholas as 'the tragedies.' It appears that this is a calculated attempt to subliminally soften the events; Sheila was guilty, but she was also suffering from severe mental health issues and so the deaths were tragedies, not the savage murders of four people including two six-year-old boys. It remains a brutal truth however, that even if Sheila were guilty of the crimes, her victims were all still, in fact, murdered and to call it anything else seems disingenuous.

Another prominent aspect of the campaign is the need to clear up confusion and within it an interesting phenomenon is the constant denial or justification of the stories which have become synonymous with the story of Jeremy's personality and actions in the days following the deaths of his family; the chat about the Porsche, choosing not to ring 999, having Crispy the dog put down, telling dirty jokes at the funeral and partying in the South of France before his eventual arrest to name but a few. What is interesting is that it becomes apparent that rebuttals stem from one source of information only: Jeremy himself. He, it could be argued, is not an impartial source.

This becomes clear during, for example, a series of podcast episodes dedicated to answering frequently asked questions about the case which concentrate not on the facts or evidence but on Jeremy's behaviour. Over several episodes they seek to answer several questions such as 'What is Jeremy Bamber really like? Did he wear make-up and dress up on the farm? Did he go on an expensive holiday to France and indulge in sex, drugs and drink? Why didn't he call 999?'[12]

The team do tend to discuss Jeremy as if they have known him since childhood and were first-hand witnesses to certain events and as such explain with great confidence how wonderful his and Sheila's relationship was when they were growing up, how much he did or didn't drink and have sex during his stay in St Tropez with Brett Collins and that he categorically did not dress up as Adam Ant while driving a tractor around the farm, describing such allegations as ridiculous. At the very least it seems ironic that the source of the information used to disprove the 'lies' about Jeremy is, well Jeremy.

Lastly, while almost certainly unintentional, the team do tend to contradict themselves. During a brief correspondence with the author and in response to the suggestion that the campaign team can sometimes seem to be rather overconfident and bordering on delusional about the efficacy of their arguments, Philip explains: 'I would say that we always try not to overstate our views in public. We only describe something as "proven" if we have evidence that we believe would prove the matter, beyond a reasonable doubt, in court. If we are not one hundred per cent sure about an issue, and there are many of these, we will always say "we believe that ...." and provide what proof we have on that subject. I accept that we occasionally might depart from this rule but, generally, that is our approach.'[13]

In what could be seen to contradict this, but which is certainly a confirmation of the confidence the team have in the evidence they have discovered, in one podcast episode Yvonne stated that 'we can absolutely one hundred per cent categorically prove that two telephone calls were made to the police' because 'it's documented from two different sources, and *that's* what happened. We know Nevill rang the police, we know Jeremy rang the police.'[14]

In one interesting episode during which Yvonne and Emma discuss the reasoning behind Jeremy choosing not to call 999 they state as fact a definitive answer to the question which in fact consists of almost complete speculation, based on what Jeremy has told them. They explain firstly that 'Jeremy knew how private his dad was' and that he didn't call 999 because he 'didn't want police turning up at the scene with the lights and sirens on' as he didn't know the 'urgency of the situation' and because he had only been asked to go and help. For all he knew, they say, he thought that by the time he got there they might all be 'sitting around the table having a cup of tea.'[15]

The only way this can be seen to make sense is if Nevill's call to Jeremy was remarkably calm, because they speculate that 'his dad didn't ask him to call the police, did he? He asked him to go over, presumably so he could help him with Sheila.' In a separate interview, Philip speculates that 'the level of concern when he made that call, it was concerning but it wasn't "Oh my God I'm about to be shot eight times, please get down here".'[16] They suggest that Nevill himself may have initially thought that he could resolve the situation himself with Jeremy's help but that then things 'may have escalated' although they do at least admit that 'we don't know' and 'can only speculate'[17] as to whether that is what happened. They do however come to the overall conclusion that essentially Nevill calmly rang Jeremy, didn't really give him any cause for concern to the point where a 999 call was warranted, but then within minutes things escalated to the point where Jeremy wanted to call the police but because he was a 'very private person' he simply called the local police station rather than 999. Of course, the elephant in the room is that this entire discussion is based solely around the fact that this phone call from Nevill *actually took place*, a fact which is corroborated by Jeremy, and Jeremy alone.

Their argument that it didn't 'ultimately make the slightest bit of difference what number he dialled'[18] as the responding police officer would have been despatched from Witham Police Station in any event might be technically true, but it doesn't take into account the *motivation* behind not calling 999. How would Jeremy know, in that moment, that a 999 call would precipitate a despatch from Witham?

During one of his several interviews, Philip puts forwards his thoughts on the whole phone call issue with the suggestion that if Jeremy was in fact guilty, that placing a call to the police was incredibly risky and that 'if he had made up the phone call from his father, it would have been the equivalent of sticking his hand in the air and saying "I did it!".'[19] He wouldn't have taken that risk, he says, because BT were in the process of digitising the lines and some of the lines in the local area were in fact recording calls; why risk this call not being logged? The counter argument to that of course is that if he did do it, he simply would have placed the call himself from within White House Farm to cover all bases. Philip ends with the statement that 'making up that phone call would have been a very, very stupid thing to have done.'[20]

The team are also prone to speculate on how other people involved in this case, in particular the police officers, should, in their opinion, have behaved. The suggestion that the rifle allegedly seen propped up in the window was in fact a vacuum cleaner hose is met with a sceptical 'you're not going to tell me that a fully trained arms officer can't tell the difference between a rifle and a vacuum cleaner!'[21] The raid team were of course highly trained officers, but this seems to work against them in the campaign team's view; they are so well trained that they should be immune to mistakes and so it becomes inconceivable to them that one might have, for example, mistaken a male body for a female one. However, Philip does say that 'Collins could easily have been mistaken in a highly stressful situation' but with the caveat that 'although, as an experienced officer, who had done two tours of duty in Northern Ireland, he would be less prone to that than other, less experienced, members of the raid team.'[22]

The team allegedly receive a fair amount of abuse, which seems a little unfair given that they are simply expressing their opinions, and they are if nothing else one hundred per cent committed to this cause. However, while abuse is never appropriate, moral eyebrows can certainly be raised at what might be described as some very distasteful practices they have partaken in. It's hard to see how they thought it would be a good idea, for example, to hold a graveside vigil for June and Nevill, with one of the campaign team reading out an emotional letter from Jeremy to his dead parents, all of which was recorded and broadcast on YouTube. Regardless of Jeremy's guilt or innocence, the motivation and purpose of this seems to be unclear, as with a bake-off event organised in which supporters were encouraged to bake cakes based on June's own recipes. If the purpose was to raise awareness for the son who is in prison convicted of murdering her it seems at the very least, bizarre. Given their dedication it seems unlikely that these actions were malicious, but it begs the question as to why they recorded the vigil and uploaded it to YouTube. If the motivation was genuine, perhaps they could have performed it peacefully and respectfully, and without cameras.

But respectfulness is regrettably missing in this campaign team in certain areas and given how firmly they believe that Jeremy is innocent it is perhaps not surprising, if jarring, to read their descriptions of the other innocent people wrapped up in this case. It appears that nobody is safe from criticism, apart from Jeremy.

Their website projects what might be described as a slightly childish tone, the most prominent example of which is their 'Liar's Lobby.' This consists of 'quotes' from people involved in the case including Stan Jones, Julie Mugford, various of Bamber's relatives and several other police officers. The quotes are deliberately fictitious, made up by the campaign team to try and put their point across while portraying the 'liars' as idiotic and hapless. For example, their take on Stan Jones reads, 'I was one of the investigating officer's [sic] on the Jeremy Bamber case. I liked a whiskey, and as luck would have it Peter Eaton let me drink a whole bottle when I collected the key evidence, the sound moderator from him.' As for Bews, first officer on the scene; 'I saw movement inside White House Farm while Jeremy Bamber was standing outside next to me. [Even though] what I saw means Jeremy Bamber is innocent, I told the 1986 trial that I might have made a mistake. I like to change my story for various media so check out this video of me lying on camera.' They go so far as to openly accuse, with Ronald Cook's entry reading, 'I had to rustle something up, so I screwed [the window catch] back on and the boys had another check on the frame and, lo and behold they found scratches on it. The jury lapped that one up as evidence of how Bamber broke in. It was a good job I had interfered with the scene, or my boys might have missed that one.'[23] It's hard to see what purpose this exercise serves aside from belittling the people to which it refers.

Of everyone involved, Julie Mugford seems to bear the brunt of this. She was just a woman scorned, they say, who falsely accused a hitman with a cast iron alibi and who simply decided that if she couldn't have Jeremy then no-one else could. Her 'Liar's Lobby quote' says 'I did get very muddled over the call times from Jeremy to me, probably because I'd been smoking pot that night. The police advised me not to tell the jury about that.' They are often scathing about Julie on a very personal level, claiming that she was not a reliable witness due to the fact that she is a 'one woman crime spree'[24] based, it appears on the cheque fraud and her part in the Osea Road burglary. She wanted to be a teacher, and they often make much of the fact that she would not have secured a job in education if she had been convicted of the crimes from which she secured immunity, they say, in return for her damning testimony. In what seems irrelevant to Jeremy's guilt or innocence, they describe her as coming 'from a working class background' and that 'as Jeremy came from a more privileged background Julie must have felt she'd done very well on the social scale as she was dating the good-looking, intelligent, wealthy and public-school educated Jeremy' and at one point suggest that she should have been pleased to have 'bagged such a catch.'[25]

We are led to believe that everyone else involved in this horrendous occurrence was at best benign and at worst corrupt while not a word can be said against Jeremy, but surely reality is more complex than that. Even if Jeremy was innocent, it doesn't mean that he never did any of the awful things he is accused of, taunting his mother with rats or cheating on several girlfriends, for example. However, the campaign team seem compelled to whitewash over any negative behaviour to convince everyone of Jeremy's upstanding values, in order to shore up their assertions of innocence. It might even be true to say that it would give more credence to their campaign if they were a little less blinkered about Jeremy's idealised image and admitted that he was not perfect.

So, what are their motivations in campaigning for Jeremy? One of the campaign teams patrons, Dr Dennis Eady, Director of Cardiff University Law School Innocence Project has been an active campaigner on miscarriage of justice issues for twenty years with South Wales against Wrongful Conviction (formerly South Wales Liberty). During an interview with the author, he explains that for him, there is simply nothing left upstanding in the prosecution's case, taking into account the doubt which has been raised over the silencer evidence, or lack of, and of Julie Mugford's testimony, both of which were the cornerstones of the prosecution's case. Of the former, he says 'it is now established that there was more than one silencer, exhibits were mixed up, the relatives tampered with these exhibits before going to the police and none of Sheila's DNA was ever found in the silencer. Also the paint scratches were not in the original photos – highly suggestive that they were made by the police to fabricate evidence – and experts have examined photographs of the wounds and concluded there was no silencer on the weapon'. Of the latter, he says that 'Mugford's first made-up story was disproved so she made up another one (what kind of evidence is that!), she went to the police after an acrimonious breakup with Jeremy, she had potential charges of theft and fraud dropped for assisting the police, she gave accounts about the number of shots and positioning of the bodies which were not only inaccurate but reflected the same error in the newspapers (in other words it came from the papers not Jeremy) and then she was paid £25,000 to sell her lies to the News of the World'.

In answer to the question as to why West or Bonnett has never once suggested they or anyone else spoke with Nevill Bamber on 7 August 1985, Eady speculates they may simply have forgotten, or more likely that their 'evidence has been sidelined as the relatives and police gradually constructed a case against Jeremy.' Developing the theme of police incompetence; to the question as to why the entire force would suddenly change their mind when they originally thought it was a murder-suicide and then decide to frame Jeremy, his answer is that it could just be one police officer trying to assert themselves with everyone then following suit or, more specifically, 'a case of the relatives putting pressure on the police, a new officer in charge taking over with a fixed belief about what happened and hence constructing evidence in that framework and directing or influencing his team accordingly.' He goes on to explain that this is 'sometimes referred to as Groupthink, or Case Construction and Tunnel vision' which is 'well recognised in policing and other organisations where people follow certain theories which may be unsubstantiated by evidence, excluding anything that does not fit the theory.'

He doesn't therefore claim that the police necessarily lied, but more that they have come to believe that Jeremy is guilty in the face of evidence which proves otherwise. He concedes that the 999 call at 6.09 am hasn't yet been confirmed but that the CCRC will hopefully do so, which, in the end of course, they did not. Does he really think that Sheila was lying prone on the floor and then suddenly got up and ran upstairs when again, not one of the police who were in attendance that day corroborate this? He agrees that while it is far-fetched, it is still plausible as 'the original pathologist stated that the first shot would not necessarily have been fatal and therefore it is entirely plausible that she shot herself twice'.[26]

He goes on to say that a common occurrence in miscarriages of justice is that 'more and more' evidence keeps appearing, and that they have witnessed this very phenomenon in Jeremy's case. Whilst one argument against this is that more *evidence* doesn't necessarily keep appearing but rather that new interpretations are placed on existing evidence, Yvonne explains her view of this in a separate podcast episode. In what she describes as a drip feed of small and apparently insignificant pieces of information gradually forming the bigger picture, she explains how she has concluded that Sheila had only been shot once when the police discovered her body. She might, for example, find one statement where an officer reports seeing a single wound on Sheila and then later, she might find another, and then another, and gradually she realises what is going on is that Sheila only had one bullet wound when she was found as she now has six separate statements stating she was discovered with a single bullet wound in her neck before 9.00 am.

The problem with this is twofold; firstly, it ignores the evidence of other people who clearly state they saw two bullet wounds on Sheila when her body was discovered and contradicts their own theory that she was lying on the floor in the kitchen as the result of the first non-fatal shot, which if true means that two shots would have been apparent when she was finally found. Secondly this somehow segues into a frankly bizarre theory that if she only had one wound when she was discovered, the only explanation therefore is one of the policemen at the scene shot her by mistake while taking part in a training exercise, the theory being that the second shot was made not by Sheila or Jeremy but by a member of the raid team. In a podcast interview Philip admitted that the second bullet appeared to have been made by someone standing above Sheila which of course would be 'extremely prejudicial' to Jeremy if true and so it seems the only way out of this is to assert that someone at the crime scene shot her.

In a slightly convoluted explanation, Philip says that Malcolm Fletcher based his opinion that the shot was fired with a moderator using the *second* shot. If the police shot Sheila by mistake as he asserts, then this shot must have been done without the moderator (because they were not used on the police weapons), meaning that Fletcher is wrong, and if he's wrong about that, then the rest of his testimony can't be believed, or as Philip put it, 'his expertise in this area is totally worthless.'[27] This of course only stands up if his theory of an accidental gunshot by the police is true.

Philip goes on to explain his theory that Taff Jones knew that Sheila was responsible because he was aware right from the beginning of the 999 call, the rifle in the window, and that she had only been shot once. He was then, he says, 'part of the cover up' and was put in a very difficult position when the second enquiry started because he 'couldn't come out and say my mate Montgomery told me they'd made a complete cock up and managed to shoot her accidentally themselves.' He should have come clean then but 'for whatever reason chose not to.'[28]

The campaign is often bolstered by 'ifs.' *If* the police accidentally shot Sheila then Fletcher's testimony is wrong. *If* the police had taken Sheila's temperature on arrival it *might* have shown that she had only just died. *If* there were digitised call logs (there were not) then they *might* have shown that there were two calls. '*If* that rifle was in that window there is no other explanation other than that Sheila committed suicide.' So, *if* Taff Jones was so adamant that Sheila had done it, would he really have kept quiet about his fellow officers accidentally shooting her in the neck?

The wider family, or at least David, don't appear to hold any animosity towards those who follow Jeremy's campaign team, but simply lament 'All I can say is that, very sadly, they have been misled.' Ainsley, on the other hand, is blunter. 'It really does escape me why Bamber's supporters pursue these nonsensical suggestions that keep coming out of his followers' mouths. It's costing us, you and I, the taxpayers a lot of money this. The lawyers are doing ok…'[29]

Mental Gymnastics

The Oxford English Dictionary describes a conspiracy theory as 'the theory that an event or phenomenon occurs as a result of a conspiracy between interested parties.'[1] Most that we recognise in popular culture are far-fetched to say the least, for example anti-vaxxers, 9-11 deniers, flat earthers and moon landing sceptics to name but a few. More recently, royal theories have emerged from those who believe that Meghan Markle faked both of her pregnancies, or that Prince William murdered his love rival and then kept the Princess of Wales captive away from the public eye (while she was actually recovering from cancer) or, unbelievably, that he also murdered her, a theory which didn't even go away after she reappeared, with claims that she was AI generated. However, the description could apply to many of the campaign team's theories in a far less extreme fashion; that the family colluded to frame Jeremy to keep their inheritance, and that the Essex Police colluded not only amongst themselves but also with the family to the same ends.

Their explanations of some of the other points may more accurately be described using the more modern term 'mental gymnastics' which, despite sounding rather athletic and positive, is used to describe arguments that involve convoluted explanations in order to prove a point or perhaps win an argument. In doing so one might discount a more simple or rational explanation which contradicts but goes hand in hand with the theory of Occam's razor, which states that of two competing theories, the simpler explanation of an entity is to be preferred. Just because it's a theory doesn't mean it is always true of course, and there will always be exceptions, but it is one which is often cited when discussing true crime; essentially, it's usually the more simple and obvious set of circumstances which is correct.

Of course this can apply to both sides of the argument; while it might be tempting to say that, for example, the idea that Sheila was unconscious downstairs, suddenly gained consciousness and then ran upstairs and shot herself in direct contradiction to what the raid team suggest is far less likely than the alternative; that Collins mistook Nevill for a female and this mistake was recorded in the call log. Conversely, one could say that the original, simple explanation that Sheila, with a history of psychosis, shot her family and then herself is far more plausible than the elaborate ruse that Jeremy is said to have come up with to cover his tracks and murder his entire family. Dr Eady describes this as the Agatha Christie effect; that some people just want to uncover a plot much more sinister and potentially exciting than the dull truth. Then one starts to think about this in the context of a force-wide conspiracy involving dozens of separate police officers hell-bent on framing a man they had never met before for murder, and the whole thing turns full circle again. However, Eady again reiterates here that this might be explained by the aforementioned fact that police officers tend to follow orders and 'may not be encouraged to question the senior officer'. As he says, '1980s policing had its faults!' and that they 'may well have ended up chasing the wrong goal' which is what he is convinced happened in Jeremy's case.

Over the years, the defence and campaign team have presented a mix of arguments, some offering plausible explanations supporting Jeremy's innocence, and others veering into conspiracy territory, relying heavily on mental gymnastics to be convincing. There is the aforementioned claim that Sheila was unconscious downstairs, that she still had wet blood running down her neck when she was found and, contrary to reports did have dirty feet. There's the allegation that a suicide note written by Sheila was found with the Bible, but that Mike Ainsley took it home with him and destroyed it.

Next there is the idea of ritual cleansing; the campaign team's one shot at explaining away the silencer, if the evidence were to prove that it was in fact used; she could have taken the silencer off and then cleaned herself up before shooting herself without it. And then of course the idea that a police officer accidentally shot her in the neck right next to the initial bullet wound, to explain away the fact that there were two. Also, in terms of the bullet, they have focused on the description of it as fragmented, suggesting that the original bullet, according to Vanezis, was fractured, but that in court it was described as whole. This appears to be irrelevant until we realise that they are suggesting that the bullet produced at trial was a substitute, which had been fired through a silencer, in order to substantiate the prosecution's assertion that the silencer was on the gun when Sheila was shot.

And of course, because these theories are apparently borne out of alleged evidence, they will inevitably be treated with a certain amount of reverence in online forums dedicated to discussing the case. There are two particularly fascinating forums dedicated to the discussion of the Jeremy Bamber case which are known colloquially as the 'Blue Forum' and the 'Red Forum' (named, it seems, because of the colour theme of each website as opposed to anything more cryptic). While they are not affiliated with the campaign team in any way, some members do of course agree wholeheartedly with their views.

The Blue Forum is dedicated mainly to the Bamber case and 'has been set up to allow a free and open discussion about the case of Jeremy Bamber and other high-profile cases.' The main 'Jeremy Bamber Case Discussion' has, at the time of writing, racked up over four-hundred and sixty-three thousand posts on a huge number of subjects with threads entitled, 'More and more people are believing that cops shot Sheila Caffell at least once', 'Essex Police framed Jeremy Bamber' and 'Confirmation that Sheila Caffell used the rifle at time of shootings.'[2] Clearly, this is a forum which believes mainly in Jeremy's innocence.

The Red Forum is, confusingly, a sub forum on a UK justice site dedicated to discussing miscarriages of justice; confusing, as this is most definitely a forum leaning towards those who are convinced of Jeremy's guilt, and therefore safe to assume that most don't believe that a miscarriage of justice has taken place. Since its first thread in March 2012, there have been over forty-three thousand posts and in contrast to the Blue Forum, includes threads such as; 'Multiple reasons why Sheila Caffell is innocent, and Jeremy Bamber is guilty,' 'More disappointment looming for Bamber?' and 'Top UK murder detective reviews the Bamber case: verdict guilty!'[3]

However, the set-up is not as black and white as it appears. Several posters and some of the senior moderators on the Red Forum are supporters of Jeremy. As is to be expected in a case which garners such emotional responses, there are plenty of futile arguments to be had within these pages. However, there is mostly a running theme and on further inspection patterns start to emerge: the Blue Forum discuss ways in which they can interpret the evidence to prove Jeremy innocent, and the Red Forum looks at said discussions and condescends from afar, pitying the poor fools who carry on with their futile quest.

Discussions on the Red Forum tend to lean more towards proving Sheila's innocence, rather than Jeremy's guilt, heading with the main arguments that she was not physically capable of shooting the gun or overpowering her father and that she cannot have committed suicide due to the fact that she had been shot twice in her neck and the gun had a silencer on it when it was fired, and the silencer evidence and so on. Even some of his detractors may admit that the evidence against Jeremy was circumstantial, which may be why the focus tends to be on Sheila's innocence. Therefore, arguments against Jeremy tend to focus on his behaviour; many believe that he's a narcissist, a master manipulator and motivated by greed.

Arguably, Jeremy's supporters have a great deal more to gain by discussing the minutiae of the case and coming up with their own theories as to why Jeremy is innocent, and for them, the approach is the opposite to their rivals. They will tend to focus on Sheila's behaviour and mental illness rather than the forensics and put more emphasis on the lack of physical evidence against Jeremy. In a nutshell, detractors will try and prove Sheila's innocence, his supporters will try and prove her guilt.

It seems there is actually a universal understanding that discussion will not change the other side's point of view; one says their interest is 'a diversion in the main from other things and I have no interest in changing anyone's mind' and another says of supporters, 'I guess they are on here trying to change opinion about Bamber (but sadly for them failing miserably as one thing forums has taught me, once you've adopted a position on any given subject you are unlikely to have your opinion changed by arguing the toss with other posters).'[4]

Discussion is certainly something the forums do well; the supporters on the Blue Forum will debate a wide range of points, including 'Are JB's real parents the REAL parents? (a question as to whether Jeremy's real father who put him up for adoption was in fact his biological father), 'Sheila's Feet' (an in-depth discussion about how clean her feet were or should/shouldn't have been when she was found) and 'Incident where Nevill is punched in the face by Peter Eaton?' (which includes the observation that the family 'sound like a right bunch'). Lastly, in what seems to sum up the forum, someone started a thread entitled 'What make, and model was Jeremy's phone?' to which someone replies, quite poignantly, 'I'm not quite sure of the point of this thread.' In an echo of this, another poster sums up the essence of true crime debate perfectly; 'the reality is that although everybody has opinions on JB's guilt or innocence [nobody] was there that night, nobody has seen ALL the evidence, and nobody can say with absolute certainty that JB is 100% guilty or 100% innocent.'[5]

Some take the idea of police corruption one step further, suggesting that Taff Jones's death was not an accident, but the result of the police's need to keep him quiet, that his wife had subsequently been silenced by 'intimidation with menaces' and one poster worryingly suggesting they were planning to find his family and ask them to prove to them that they witnessed his death and therefore prove it was an accident. One post in particular seems to sum up the atmosphere on either forum; in reaction to a post claiming that murderers can be identified by their blood group ('Blood Type Os tend to be the leaders and As are more shy. I could hazard a guess at how your grandparents died from their blood type but we're getting off topic') the reply is succinct: 'With all due respect Steve but that's quite simply bonkers.'[6]

While these people are essentially faceless, over the years the campaign has garnered significant real-world support from some relatively well-known faces and journalists. Conversely, there is also a large following represented through various podcasts and documentaries who very much believe that the right verdict was reached, and that Jeremy is deservedly where he belongs, behind bars.

One of the more well-known faces who believe Jeremy to be innocent is ex-policeman journalist Mark Williams-Thomas who was behind the making of a documentary called *Bamber – The New Evidence* which aired on ITV in 2012 and which put forward several of the campaign team theories and expanded on one in particular; further research carried out using pigs' skin using a recently fired rifle to prove that the marks on Nevill's back were made by the AGA handle rather than the rifle. This in and of itself doesn't really prove either way whether Sheila or Jeremy was the attacker but rather throws more doubt on whether, or not, the silencer was used at all during the attacks. *Crimes that Shook Britain* is another documentary which is often cited as the catalyst for believing that a miscarriage of justice had occurred, perhaps because it states as fact that Nevill placed a call to the police, that one dead male and one dead female were discovered in the kitchen, and that a 999 call was made from within the house.

Peter Tatchell is a very well-known campaigner for social justice, heading up The Peter Tatchell Foundation (PTF) which, according to its website 'seeks to promote and protect the human rights of individuals, communities and nations, in the UK and internationally, in accordance with established national and international Human Rights law.' Peter has become a staunch supporter of Jeremy's campaign, based mostly around the appeal for non-disclosed evidence to be released. In 2017 he wrote to the Chief Constable of Essex, Stephen Kavanagh 'urging him to comply fully with three court orders to make available to Jeremy Bamber's legal team hundreds of pieces of evidence that Essex Police have failed to disclose for 32 years. Shockingly, some evidence has been destroyed, despite court orders to hand it over to the defence.' Again in 2021 he wrote to Chief Constable Ben-Julian Harrington with the same request and in which he says 'I cannot say whether Jeremy Bamber is guilty or innocent. But I know that denying him access to relevant evidence at his trial and appeals is a grave injustice. He has a legal right to this evidence. Without it, he may not have had a fair trial, and his conviction may be unsafe.' The evidence which the campaign team say is being withheld was requested in this letter as:

1. *Original manuscript/handwritten logs by Malcolm Bonnett (civilian telephone operator at police HQ) and PC West from 03:26am (Nevill Bamber's call) and 03:36 am (Jeremy Bamber's call), on 7 August 1985.*
2. *Audio recordings of:*
    - *PC West's calls to HQ operator Malcolm Bonnett*
    - *All radio traffic referred to by Malcolm Bonnett*
    - *The raid team's open microphones*

3. *Original situation report made by PS Bews following the sighting of someone alive in White House Farm that was seen through a bedroom window prompting him to request firearms assistance.*
4. *Original statements made on 07.08.85 by PS Bews, and PC Myall who saw movement in a bedroom window of White House Farm.*
5. *DI Kenneally's 06.09.85 report following his investigation stating "The evidence indicated that Sheila was responsible."*
6. *DI Kenneally's statement made post-trial for the Dickinson enquiry (1986).*
7. *PC Milbank's pocket book recording all his monitoring of the telephone line at White House Farm from 06:09 onwards on 07.08.85.*
8. *The audio recording of the 999 call made from White House Farm at 06:09am on 7 August 1985.*
9. *The original handwritten statements and pocket book entries from the first case investigation of murder/suicide SC/688/85 including:*
    - *PC 7975 David Bishop statements dated 14.09.85*
    - *DI Cook statements dated 07.08.85.*
    - *DS 219 Davidson statements dated 09.08.85*
    - *DCI Jones statements dated 07.08.85*
    - *PS Mildenhall statements dated 18.09.85*
    - *Inspector Montgomery statements dated 20.08.85*
    - *Chief Inspector Wright statements dated 09.09.85*
    - *PS 36 Bews statements dated 18.09.85*
    - *PC 1902 Cracknell statements dated 17.09.85*
    - *PC 721 East statements*
    - *DC Henderson statements*
    - *PC 1046 Maunder statements*
    - *PC 721 Spelman statements*
    - *PC 1445 Reed statements*
    - *PC 366 Shoulders statements*

10. *The complete set of blood charts relative to the silencers, and Sheila Caffell's nightdress.*
11. *All photographs taken of all the rooms in White House Farm including those containing firearms and all telephones in situ.*
12. *All photographs of the silencer and the sound moderator.*
13. *The exhibit label for the silencer for rifle SBJ/1.*
14. *The General Examination Record (Holmes Box 12/34) for the paint sample RM/1.*
15. *The diagrams created by Andrew Palmer on 11.09.85 of the sound moderator DB/1.*
16. *The General Examination Record of Louise Floate dated 12.09.85.*
17. *The pocket notebook of DS Robert Cook.*
18. *All forensic scientist's pre-trial handwritten statements, lab reports and post-trial DCI Dickinson enquiry interviews pertaining to the sound moderator(s).*
19. *Public Interest Immunity file on Julie Mugford (Jeremy Bamber's girlfriend at the time of the killings) referring to a 'deal' with the Crown Prosecution Service in exchange for immunity from prosecution for five criminal offences, three of which were unknown to the jury. Plus, disclosure of the Essex Police file on the £25,000 News of the World deal, agreed to in November/December 1985 (pre-trial) by Julie Mugford via her solicitors.*
20. *Sheila Caffell's medical/psychiatric records referring to her conversations with her psychiatrist where she informs him, she was afraid she would kill her children. Plus Sheila's diaries during periods where she had psychotic episodes (1983 and 1985).*[7]

Harrington's reply appeared to confirm that these documents do in fact exist as he explained in clear terms that 'throughout [this appeal] process my investigators have assisted the court providing documents as required to do so to ensure we adhere to our legal obligations' before confirming that 'at this time, I will not be authorising any further material to Mr Bamber's solicitors' thus sparking a post on the PTF website named 'Essex Police admit suppressing Jeremy Bamber evidence.'[8] At the time of writing, no further evidence has been forthcoming, although it seems the motivation here is more the principle of disclosing the information rather than the expectation that what is held within it will necessarily prove anything one way or another.

Jeremy also boasts a certain amount of political support; former MP Andrew Hunt is a strong advocate of his innocence and has taken part in several documentaries and interviews about the case. He is clearly very much on board with the corruption angle, as he states quite unequivocally in one such interview that 'it looks as though the police were in league with the family.'[9] Jeremy was also the subject of a parliamentary question by MP David Davis in 2021, 'to ask the Secretary of State for Justice, on what (a) public interest grounds and (b) risk assessment evidence Jeremy Bamber has been denied transfer to a lower category prison status.' The answer was essentially that 'HMPPS has an obligation to protect the public by preventing escape of the most dangerous offenders. All category A prisoners must be held within a high security prison.'[10]

Members of the JBIC are often seen as guests on YouTube or other productions, not least appearing on the morning radio show of Sonia Poulton, a journalist, broadcaster, social commentator & documentary filmmaker who, according to her website, worked with the Spice Girls and was 'instrumental in creating their iconic nicknames'[11] and appears regularly debating on ITV's flagship show *This Morning.* Sonia is fully on board and suitably outraged at the alleged miscarriage of justice put to her by the campaign team, as is Emma Kenny, a TV psychologist and presenter, posting a video of her in conversation with the team, subsequently following up with a three-episode account of her own personal views on why Jeremy Bamber is innocent.

Perhaps understandably, the team are generally only seen in conversation with interviewers who agree with them and very rarely in any actual debate in which they are challenged, with very minor exceptions. During an appearance on *Crime Suspect* in February 2024 hosted by Peter Bleksley, a former Scotland Yard detective, Philip was a guest alongside Matt Harris, a filmmaker who also believes in Jeremy's guilt and Jo Hemmings, a behavioural psychologist who had clearly been brought in for balance and who stated that she believed Jeremy to have all the traits of someone with narcissistic personality disorder; perhaps reasonably, given that she has never met him, Philip dismisses this as supposition. However, Bleksley, when asking for an explanation about the call logs is seemingly sceptical as to the assertion that they refer to two separate calls, putting it to Philip and Matt that this evidence was very likely the result of human error and that it was ultimately strong enough to convince a jury to convict him. Turning his back on them both before they had a chance to counter an answer earned him a rather bemused look from Philip who appears not to have much experience of being challenged. Interestingly, Matt Harris accuses Essex Police of using 'human error to sell their narrative'[12] perhaps very much in an echo of the way the campaign team use police corruption to sell theirs.

True crime podcasts, of course, go wild for the White House Farm murders and as is often the case, the ones who maintain his innocence seem to use as reference the information given out by the campaign team, taking what they hear as fact and subsequently these numerous episodes heard independently are very compelling. Taken at face value it seems absolutely ludicrous that Jeremy is still behind bars; if Nevill did make a phone call, and police were chatting with Sheila inside the farm, following which someone spoke to her on the phone during a 999 call then of course he should be released. If police officers really did find her body on the floor of the kitchen and then again when she had finally killed herself upstairs then yes, she is guilty.

However, one podcast, *The White House Farm Murders* hosted by Kaiesha Page is arguably one of the most balanced, perhaps because of the obviously extensive research on which it is based but more so because Kaiesha admits that the initial motivation behind starting it was in fact to demonstrate Jeremy's innocence. She was friendly with the campaign team and fully on board with them, with her 'aha' moment being the Mark Williams-Thomas documentary at which she started to disbelieve her previous conceptions of the case, followed swiftly by watching the dramatisation based on the book by Carol Ann Lee which she said initially appalled her and motivated her to start her podcast to assert Jeremy's innocence. However, it only took two or three weeks to realise that the evidence wasn't quite as compelling as she had first thought as 'you've only got to delve below the surface to realise that it's quite a simple case.'[13] Lots of people, she says, discover the case from this angle, including the aforementioned author and now friend of hers Carol Ann Lee, who also initially believed in Jeremy's innocence.

Therefore it seems that this is a case in which people are prone to changing their minds about what they believe, with some convinced by the veracity of the verdict and then having their eyes opened to the real truth of his innocence, or the opposite; some that believe the assertions that there is cast iron proof of his innocence until they delve further into it and realise that these claims are perhaps less cast iron than the campaign team would have them believe. Kaiesha belongs to the latter and the more she researched the case, the more she realised that the 'evidence' of which she had been convinced was becoming less and less plausible. The episodes of her podcast which are currently available are incredibly in depth and inevitably include echoes of her previous opinions; she has interviewed several key people including the campaign team, Brett Collins, Chris Bews, Police Constable West and Terry Mullins who took Jeremy's polygraph test which he says proves his innocence. One episode is dedicated to her interview with the author Carol Ann Lee at Crime Con.

Perhaps because she has come to her own conclusions over time, Kaiesha is very logical and level-headed when it comes to the case and is still astonished at although somewhat admiring of the dedication, if not the mental gymnastics of the campaign team. While she was interviewing them, one member suggested that such was her commitment to the cause that 'even if Jeremy Bamber said he was guilty she would ask him to show her the evidence that he was.'[14] She describes it as almost cult-like, necessitating the belief that the scale of the cover up required would involve not only the entire Essex Police Force but every Home Secretary since 1985. With regards to the alleged non-disclosure of evidence which is held under Public Interest Immunity (PII) being portrayed as something illicit or corrupt, her view is that PII covers a whole multitude of cases, particularly those involving children. Certain documents surrounding the Dunblane massacre for example, are withheld under PII, this does not mean that there is anything suspicious in them not being released.

So, while a plethora of people are convinced either way of Jeremy's guilt or innocence, it's not just reserved for those web sleuths chatting about it online. The most recent documentary about the case, at the time of writing, was produced by Louis Theroux who has stated in interviews that 'there are "legit" people who think Bamber is serving a whole-life prison term for a crime he didn't carry out. Across the board you'll find people who believe there were serious problems with the case, in terms of how it was investigated and how it was prosecuted,' he told Sky News. 'There are things that are quite hard to explain on both sides.'[15]

And so, while he himself perhaps understandably sits on the fence, he makes his belief very clear that this team of people campaigning for Jeremy's innocence are not a small band of eccentrics or fanatics. As he puts it, 'A lot of them are legit people. There are a lot of prominent journalists who would say they would feel Bamber is innocent. It's not by any means a kind of fringe belief."[16]

MISCARRIAGE OR JUSTICE?

Stranger Things Have Happened

It's clear that some cases are more contentious than others and indeed some where we will never know what truly happened. But what happens when a case ends in a conviction which is potentially unsafe with both sides of the argument campaigning vociferously that their viewpoint is correct and then suddenly the missing piece of evidence appears to prove beyond reasonable doubt one way or another as has been claimed by Jeremy's campaign team?

When a case is 'proven' does it leave campaigners feeling exhilarated at having been proved right or humiliated at having to concede defeat? Or would they continue to argue their point in the face of overwhelming evidence? Jeremy's case does not stand alone, and it's certainly not a purely contemporary phenomenon. It's interesting to look back at two historic cases which may or may not follow the same route as this one, proving that modern forensics don't necessarily put the matter to rest once and for all.

Proven Guilty

On 22 August 1961, Michael Gregsten and his mistress, Valerie Storie were subjected to a horrific ordeal, culminating in Michael's murder; Valerie would survive but was paralysed from the waist down.

They had spent the day together, ending with a visit to their favourite pub at around 8.00 pm. They then headed to a 'Lovers Lane' spot which they often visited, and it was here they were held up at gun point by a man who claimed to have been 'on the run' and was 'a desperate man.'[1] They were held hostage in their car until around 11.30 pm, when the man instructed Gregsten to drive the car towards Slough.

By 1.30 am they were travelling along the A6 from Luton to Bedford; their kidnapper wanted to sleep and eventually they pulled into a layby named 'Deadman's Hill.' The car ended up parked on a concrete strip parallel to the A6, facing Luton, with its lights turned off. Gregsten was in the driver's seat, the man sat with Valerie in the back.

Before sleeping, the man first had to tie up his victims; having used Gregsten's tie to bind Valerie's wrists, he asked Gregsten to pass him a laundry bag from the front of the car to the back; as he lifted it over the seat, Gregsten was shot twice in the head and died instantly. The man told Valerie that he had shot because 'He frightened me. He moved too quick. I got frightened.'[2] The man then sexually assaulted Valerie in the back of the car. He forced her to help drag Gregsten's body out of the front, and to start the car and show him how to use the gears. He then shot at her before getting into the car and driving off in the direction of Luton.

It wasn't until 6.45 am that a passer-by, John Kerr, discovered the crime scene; he called the police and an ambulance and while he waited Valerie told him her version of events and he jotted them down and handed them to the police when they arrived. By the following day Valerie's description of the assailant was in all the papers based on her statements to the police, and to John Kerr. They all generally agreed that the assailant was around 5'6", medium build with deep set brown eyes.

On 23 August, the car was discovered around seventy miles away; two witnesses had seen it being driven erratically and got a good look at the driver. The following day, the murder weapon and ammunition were found under the back seat of a 36A bus; Mr Cooke, who discovered them, confirmed that they had not been there the previous day, placing the suspect on the bus sometime on 24 August. Working on the routes the bus had taken that day, it was established that the gun must have been left either early in the morning somewhere between Peckham and Kilburn, or later in the afternoon in South London.

Police found themselves with two main suspects: Peter Alphon and James Hanratty. Alphon had been suggested to the police by the manager of a hotel he had been staying in as another guest had been concerned by his erratic behaviour. Hanratty had apparently been suggested by the widow of Michael Gregsten; according to accounts she encountered him in a café and having seen him, she announced 'that's the man. He fits the description. But it's more than that. I've got an overpowering feeling that it's him.'

The description she was referring to were two identikit pictures which had just been released, based on eyewitness testimony. Identikit was in its infancy; both pictures depicted a dark eyed man; Alphon had hazel eyes, Hanratty's were blue. There is some confusion about Valerie's testimony, as she now described her attacker as having 'icy blue, saucer like eyes.'[3]

On 24 September, Valerie Storie attended an identity parade which included Peter Alphon and did not pick him out. On 13 October, Hanratty was picked out of an identity parade by the two witnesses of the erratically driven car, followed by Valerie Storie on the following day. On 14 October Hanratty was charged with the murder of Michael Gregsten. Following trial in February 1962, Hanratty was found guilty, and was hanged at Bedford on 4 April 1962.

It's not hard to see why journalist Paul Foot, from whose book *Who Killed Hanratty?* the above series of events was put together, campaigned for years to prove Hanratty's innocence, and heavily implied that Peter Alphon was the real killer the police should have apprehended. On the face of it there seem to be many inconsistencies in the story and the details make it a classic for armchair detectives to discuss; why did Valerie change her description of the man from having brown eyes to blue? Did the identikit pictures resemble Hanratty, or were they more similar to Alphon? Did the couple get pulled over at gun point, or did they offer the man a lift?

There had also been other areas of contention, firstly surrounding the goings on at the Vienna Hotel. On 11 September, cartridge cases which turned out to be from the murder weapon were discovered in Room 24 of the Vienna Hotel in Maida Vale. Police confirmed that the bedroom had been occupied the night before the murders by a Mr J. Ryan. They also discovered however, that Alphon had stayed at the hotel on the night of the murders, although in a different room and under the name of Durrant.

Statements were given by the assistant manager of the hotel, William Nudds, who was in fact a notorious police informer; the implication being that he could not be trusted. He gave three statements regarding Alphon; the first implicated him, the second retracted, and the third implicated him again. Alphon was however released without charge when Valerie Storie failed to pick him out in the identity parade. Nudds also told police that he had given guest Mr J Ryan, believed to be Hanratty, directions on request and told him to head for the 36 bus route, where the cartridges were eventually found.

Hanratty insisted he had been in Liverpool on 22 August; he had left the Vienna hotel and walked to Paddington where he travelled up by train and spent the afternoon and early evening in the city, still travelling under the name of Ryan. The reason for his trip was to sell some stolen jewellery; he deposited it at the left luggage and was able to describe in detail an attendant with a 'withered or turned hand.'[4]

He then visited a sweet shop to ask for directions to find Carlton Road which was where he was supposed to meet the fence. He never made the meeting as he got lost, but a Mrs Dinwoodie from the sweet shop identified Hanratty from one photograph but there was some confusion as to whether this sighting had taken place on 21 or 22 August.

However, he followed up with a second, alternative alibi; he says he had headed from Liverpool to Rhyl to seek out a different fence but on being unable to find him, passed his time in amusement arcades, local shops, a barbers and a café called Dixie's, staying two nights in a guest house run by landlady Grace Jones. Later in court his defence would call Jones who clearly remembered Hanratty, placing him in Rhyl while the A6 murders were taking place.

However, she was not a credible witness and was unable to pick Hanratty out in a police photograph showing his natural hair colour (he had dyed it before his trip to Rhyl) and essentially the alibi was dismissed.

The A6 Murder Committee

Paul Foot's book was 'written at the request of and with the help of the A6 Murder Committee', a group who 'sustained a vigorous campaign over many years' to prove Hanratty innocent and to clear his name; the man at the helm was businessman Jean Justice; Foot says that 'the A6 murder and what he regards as its unjust sequel has been the main motivation of Mr Justice's existence.'[5]

There were no internet forums in 1961 and, of course, the motivation of this group was a very real desire to overturn a conviction of a man they were convinced to be innocent, who had been wrongly executed for the crime. There was true justice at stake, rather than a morbid fascination with discussing the finer points of evidence and came around the time when the British public were becoming more and more uncomfortable with the idea of capital punishment.

Ruth Ellis was the last woman to be hanged in Britain having gone to the gallows in 1955, and another controversial case, that of Derek Bentley still rankled with consciences; despite not being the person to actually pull the trigger Derek, who had learning difficulties, was hanged in 1953 while Christopher Craig, the gunman, avoided the death penalty as he was only 16 years old at the time of the murder. The last execution took place in Britain in 1964, just two years after Hanratty went to the gallows.

Several celebrities also became involved in Hanratty's case, perhaps the most notable being John Lennon who, along with his wife Yoko Ono, were introduced to Hanratty's parents by a mutual friend in 1969. They took up the cause and in December of that year attended the premiere of Ringo Starr's film *The Magic Christian* carrying a banner proclaiming that 'Britain Murdered Hanratty.' Ludovic Kennedy, a prolific campaigner against miscarriages of justice and for the abolition of the death penalty was also involved in the Hanratty campaign. He had previously campaigned for both Derek Bentley and Timothy Evan's posthumous pardons; Evans was convicted of killing his infant daughter who had, in fact, been murdered by now infamous serial killer John Christie.

Proof

In 1997, advances in DNA technology allowed testing to take place on samples kept from Valerie's underwear, and from the cloth which had been wrapped around the gun, discovered on the bus. They were found to be a match for Hanratty, and in 2002 Lord Woolf, the Lord Chief Justice said the DNA evidence established Hanratty's guilt 'beyond doubt.'

Officially the case was closed. However, it seems that DNA evidence does not necessarily convince. Paul Foot's book was published in 1970, not long after Hanratty's execution but long before his guilt was proven. However, in an article from The Guardian in 2002, he explains: 'For years, those of us campaigning for Hanratty's innocence had been asking for these DNA tests but were told that no DNA could be recovered from the exhibits. In November 1997 scientists took a swab from Michael Hanratty, the dead man's brother. To the astonishment of the commission, there was a match with his DNA and a handkerchief wrapped around the murder gun when it was found after the murder, and a small square of knickers worn by Valerie Storie on the night she was raped and she and her lover, Michael Gregsten, shot.' He goes on to say that; 'The DNA findings conflicted grotesquely with the alibis. If Hanratty was guilty, as the DNA suggested, he could not have been in Liverpool and Rhyl. If he was in Liverpool and Rhyl, there must be something wrong with the DNA'.[6]

Foot never conceded to the evidence, stating that: 'James Hanratty can never be released, but as the expertise in DNA grows, perhaps scientists in the future will apply their minds to the DNA evidence in this case and seek to solve the continuing riddle of how it proved that a man who was in Rhyl managed to commit a murder near Bedford.'[7]

Valerie Storie died in 2016. Her obituary in the Telegraph says that she bore Hanratty's family no ill will, but 'she found it distasteful, however, that their belief in their son's innocence had been boosted by campaigners who had given them false hope.' She herself asserted that 'I identified the guilty man. I looked in his eyes and he looked in mine. I knew who he was, and he knew that I recognised him. I had found the guilty person.'[8]

Interestingly, Bob Woffinden a renowned journalist specialising in miscarriages of justice authored a book titled *Hanratty – The Final Verdict* and also covered the Barry George case. Given this, he might also be assumed to support Jeremy. However, according to his interview in the documentary *Murders at White House Farm – Behind Mansion Walls* he stated that his opinion of Jeremy Bamber is that 'he is a psychopath who has persuaded lots of people that he is innocent.'[9]

Proven Innocent

Australians Michael and Lindy Chamberlain already had two sons, Aidan and Reagan, when their much longed for daughter, Azaria, was born on 11 June 1980. Seasoned campers, the Chamberlains thought nothing of taking their new-born baby on a family trip to Uluru (formerly known as Ayers Rock) and so, on 11 August 1980, they set off for a much anticipated break. They set up camp on a sand dune camping area known as Sunrise Hill which offered spectacular views of Uluru at sunrise and enjoyed some climbing and sightseeing the following day.

On the evening of 12 August, the family enjoyed the traditional and beautiful observation of the rock changing colour from orange to red in the setting sun. They had become friendly with other campers and were preparing a barbecue under the stars, striking up a conversation with Greg and Sally Lowe, from Tasmania. Lindy chatted to Sally while she nursed Azaria to sleep, and then went to put her down in the tent which was pitched near the barbecue area, where Reagan was already asleep. Her son Aidan went too, worn out from a day's climbing with his dad and brother.

Lindy settled Azaria and Aidan, although Aidan then decided that he was still hungry, so he and Lindy headed back to where the food was, and Lindy continued her conversation with Sally. Another couple who had befriended the Chamberlains, Bill and Judith West, were in their tent nearby and later testified that around this time, they heard a dog growling. Just afterwards, Sally said she heard a baby cry. Lindy hadn't heard the noise, but Aidan told her he thought it sounded like his sister, and Michael agreed. Lindy went to check.

According to her testimony, Lindy saw a dingo emerge from the tent as she approached, shaking its head; she couldn't see what was in its mouth as the view of the tent was partially obscured by a low pine railing. She shouted at the animal, which ran off; she then entered the tent. The centre pole of the tent had been knocked over, and the blankets were all over the floor; there was no sign of Azaria.

'A dingo has got my baby!'[10]

What followed was a frantic search for Azaria, and the dingo. Lindy had shouted out to the others; Michael and Greg arrived at the tent first; Lindy told him that the animal had run off in the direction of Sunrise Hill, so Michael followed. He was hampered by the dark; Greg managed to get a torch from Sally and follow Michael into the bush.

At around 8.10 pm, Michael had returned to find a torch and retreated back into the bush to continue searching alongside police and rangers who had by then arrived. By now, it seemed that Michael had resigned himself to the fact that his daughter was dead, suggesting to the ranger that 'It would be probable that the dingo would kill the child immediately, wouldn't it?'[11]

Within around thirty minutes there were approximately three hundred people searching after word had spread to other campers on site. The search was in full swing under the guidance of the ranger and the search party contained policemen, campers and Aboriginal trackers. Michael did not continue to search, remaining by the tent near his wife and sons. By 11.00pm, with no sign of Azaria, the Chamberlains agreed to leave the site and spend the rest of the night in a nearby motel.

The turning point in the case came when, on 24 August, a sightseer discovered Azaria's jumpsuit around four kilometres from the camp site where she went missing. The police were immediately suspicious; firstly, they didn't believe that a dingo was capable of taking a baby and much less carrying it over that distance. They also thought that the jumpsuit did not appear to have been ripped by teeth, but rather that it had been cut with something sharp. There was no sign of the matinee jacket which Lindy said Azaria had been wearing.

The result of the first inquest into Azaria's death in December 1980, was that '[she] met her death when attacked by a wild dingo whilst asleep in the family's tent at the top camping area, Ayers Rock, shortly after 8.00 pm on 17th August 1980.'[12] However, almost a year after Azaria's disappearance, Professor James Cameron, a forensic pathologist, obtained permission to re assess the jumpsuit. On the basis of his findings Lindy was told that 'he confirms that there was no dingo involved in the disappearance of your daughter.'

There followed a quashing of the findings of the first inquest and a second inquest concluded that Lindy Chamberlain had killed her daughter by cutting her throat and disposing of the body. On 29 October 1982, following an eight-week trial, Lindy Chamberlain was found guilty of murdering her daughter, Azaria, and sentenced to life imprisonment. She would go on to suffer years of hatred at the hands of the Australian public.

In the end it was the minute scientific evidence of alleged blood found in the stairwell of her car which convicted Lindy, but the death of a British tourist four years later that led to her release. On 26 January 1986 David Brett headed up Uluru; nobody knows for sure what happened, but he must have had a fall as, on 2 February his body was found in a fairly inaccessible area between the rock and a small hill of dirt. Approximately seventy metres away, while searching the surrounding area, volunteers discovered Azaria's missing matinee jacket. It was around one hundred and fifty metres from where the jumpsuit had been found in 1980. As the position of the jacket seemed to corroborate the story that a dingo had in fact taken Azaria, a new inquiry was called for and Lindy was ultimately released more than six years after her conviction.

This case was huge news in Australia, and it appears that the country was split in its opinion of Lindy's guilt or innocence, with the apparent trend being towards believing that she is still guilty.

So, it seems that despite the evidence, it is hard to let go of a long-held belief, and, after all, can we ever truly know the truth? Could the DNA evidence in Hanratty's case have been caused by contamination? Back in the 1960s the handling of evidence would have been much less clinical than now, particularly as the prospect of DNA testing wasn't even heard of. It's quite possible that Hanratty's belongings had been stored with the other evidence which was later tested and found to contain traces of his DNA.

The evidence in Lindy's case seems much more convincing. The investigation was strongly driven by confirmation bias; finding evidence to fit a theory as they believed the idea of a dingo taking a baby was too far-fetched, whereas the idea of a loving mother calmly slitting her ten-week-old baby's throat in the front seat of her car and then returning to chat to friends at a barbecue was apparently not.

If a person is guilty or innocent of a crime, only they can ever know that fact for sure. Everyone else can only think or believe it based on the facts they are presented with. As one commenter on the Chamberlain case put it, 'No-one except Lindy will ever really know for sure if she killed her baby, but I doubt it. The dingo story still seems far-fetched, but stranger things have happened.'[13]

A Life of Less Liberty

It is not too simplistic to suggest that this entire argument comes down to one question which only Jeremy Bamber himself can answer; is he a manipulative narcissist or an innocent victim?

It becomes more complicated when questioning *why* people believe one or the other to be true. It does appear that those who believe the former base this on the evidence which has been presented; in the form of the silencer and Julie Mugford's testimony but arguably, mostly because of the negative image of Jeremy's behaviour formed by the testimony of almost everyone who came into contact with him at the time. While it's not a definitive answer, it is interesting to look at the bigger picture about how people perceive Jeremy Bamber, and the fact is that very few, if any people who knew him personally at the time of the murders believes him to be innocent. Not Colin, not the Boutflours or the Pargeter's, not the police, not anyone who worked at White House Farm and now not even his former friend Brett Collins. And therefore, the truth is that the majority of people who support his innocence are people who have met him since he has been incarcerated and so have arguably only ever met a very different Jeremy to the one who existed in 1985, who has nothing if not time on his hands, time in which he may well have perfected the kind, generous, shy and appreciative victim which the campaign team now know.

During an episode of *Faking It*, a programme dedicated to analysing the body language, linguistics and personality of convicted killers, often those who have been observed or caught out in some sort of a lie, experts Dr Cliff Lansley, a body language analyst, Professor Dawn Archer, a Professor of Linguistics and Kerry Daynes, a psychologist, analysed Jeremy. The episode concentrated mainly on his looks and behaviour during and after the funeral, with Lansley suggesting that Jeremy's show of grief was faked due to his face not utilising the muscles which naturally and instinctively show grief (essentially, he faked his pout), but Archer's analysis of a recording of Jeremy protesting his innocence was quite compelling, conceding that while Jeremy can come across as very credible, she reminds us that 'truth and credibility are not necessarily the same thing.' In response to his assertion on tape that 'you know what, I've not revealed all my hand to the CCRC' she finds this odd, suggesting that 'If I was in this position, I'd use every card I had' and understandably asks the question 'why not show your whole hand? Unless it's a game…'[1]

And so, while experts who analyse such things and who are far removed from Jeremy himself often agree with his guilt, it could be argued that the potentially susceptible may be open to manipulation by Jeremy Bamber, and he certainly does not shy away from correspondence, albeit generally only with people who believe in his innocence. It could be that this prolific letter writing is a form of manipulation which is more effective on some than others; the former begin to fight for his cause and the latter fall by the wayside.

There is no doubt that many people over the years have succumbed to Jeremy's charms, whether those charms are real or not. Some posters on the forums appear to have become members of Jeremy's inner circle in real life and build up a picture of what this involvement might be like, with one person claiming to be 'just one of a very small handful of 'constants' around him. Over the years, some slipped away but I remained and did what I could,' but describing regular phone and written contact with the prisoner abruptly coming to a halt for no apparent reason. One describes an almost romantic attachment which involved her sending him a generous monthly allowance. Both 'relationships' eventually faltered, and yet here they are still protesting his innocence on an online forum. The latter called time on the friendship when she realised she was allegedly just being used for money while another initially supported his innocence and started to correspond with him, eventually concluding that he never really gave her a straight answer to her questions. She noticed 'a pattern began to form where he would answer straightforward questions and completely avoid or sidestep the more difficult or controversial ones.' [2] There is no denying that Jeremy possesses the ability to provoke strong feelings in others, whether they be positive, or negative. Of course there is no proof that these anonymous posters are anything but fantasists living out an alternate life online; again, stranger things have happened.

Jeremy is, without doubt, articulate and personable. Through correspondence with the author his few letters portrayed a chatty character with a hint of immaturity, eager to be in contact and at times self-effacing but with a defensive edge. Perhaps inevitably and almost certainly deliberately they do not give anything of real consequence away, with the impression of giving the same carefully measured answers to repeated questions which he no doubt receives year in and year out.

Within them he, obviously, totally refutes his guilt. Understandably, he talks of his 'multiple alibis' because 'Sheila was alive in the house for hours after me and around fifty-odd cops and paramedics had arrived at the scene.' He also describes the 'various witnesses who saw Sheila moving around in the house' and that they also saw 'lights going on and off and curtains being opened and closed.' He also reminded that 'some cops talked to Sheila, she made a 999 call at 6.09 am which is well documented.'[3]

His final letter to date was scathing about this forthcoming publication. Although he says with regret that he cannot discuss the full details of the current CCRC submission as they are 'not in the public domain' he explains that he did work closely with the New Yorker in relation to the Heidi Blake's article. Of this book, he anticipates that it will 'regurgitate old, tired and false evidence from the past' but that it might be able to 'repackage some of these old lies and make something out of it.' He ends with, again, a cryptic hint of more evidence to come with the assertion that 'no-one wants to read nonsense from forty years ago, people will read new material. Thing is, this will all be in the public domain very soon, so watch this space. With every good wish, Jeremy.'

Given that he relies on such a dedicated team of supporters, it's hard to shake the feeling that the content of these letters is as much a result of him believing what they have come up with and then in turn repeating it to everyone who will listen as it is a real conviction on his part that it is true. It's almost as if his team of workers have shown him a light at the end of the tunnel to cling on to through their own fanatical drive to find answers which might not even exist and in that moment, it seems entirely plausible that he has convinced himself that it is all fact; the phone calls, Sheila running upstairs to shoot herself before being shot by an errant police officer, it's all true. And if so, it's hard now to distinguish who is the driving force behind it all. Is Jeremy manipulating his campaign team or are they the ones manipulating him?

There is a running theme in the JBIC's podcast during a series of episodes entitled *A Life of Less Liberty* in which they lament the lifetime which Jeremy's incarceration has robbed him of, and they often feature campaign team members reading out poignant essays from Jeremy himself reminiscing about his childhood and family and his regret at having missed out on so much during the forty years that he has been in prison. Despite the debate continuing, none of us can ever know for sure if we should genuinely feel sorry for the hardship he has suffered for, if true, it must be torture.

So many victims remain as a result of what happened within White House Farm on 7 August 1985; not only those who died but also those who live with the memories every day. Whether or not the wider family were concerned about their inheritance is a moot point, they too lost beloved family members that night; Anne in particular thought of June and Nevill as almost surrogate parents. The team from Essex Police bore witness to the discovery of five bodies when they finally gained entry into White House Farm, two of whom were six-year-old boys. Regardless of how rigorous or disciplined their training and background may have been, they were then, and remain now, human beings, not machines.

What they discovered in White House Farm will live with them forever, and yet they and the family who loved June, Nevill, Sheila, Daniel and Nicholas live with the knowledge that a website exists, easily accessible to them and anyone else, which repeatedly refers to them as a bunch of inept liars. Julie Mugford offered to identify Daniel and Nicholas following their murders to spare their father Colin. And he of course, while arguably the remaining family member who had lost the most, is also often overlooked despite living his life in the shadow of this crime. He lost his precious sons that night, and in every way imaginable also lost their mother who he had once loved, not just in death but because of the continued shadow which is still regularly thrown over her memory.

Acknowledgements

With thanks to friends and family who have listened to endless discussions about this case, and specifically those who have given up their valuable time and specialist knowledge to answer my questions:

Retired Sergeant Andy Bone
Dr Charlotte Booth
Dr Dennis Eady
Dr Peadar O'Donohoe
Kaiesha Page
Christopher Pollard
Nick Roberts
Rachel Utley
Philip Walker
Dr Rachel Ward
Pete Watt

References

Publications

Caffell, C. 1995: *In Search of the Rainbow's End*. Hodder & Stoughton.

Crispin, K. 1987: *The Dingo Baby Case*. Lion Publishing.

Foot, P. 1973: *Who Killed Hanratty?* Panther.

Harrison, P. 1988: *Deviant. Jeremy Bamber and the White House Murders*. Vertical Editions.

Lee, CA. 2016: *The Murders at White House Farm*. Pan MacMillan.

Lomax, S. 2020: *Jeremy Bamber. Evil, Almost Beyond Belief*. The History Press.

Powell, C. 1994: *Murder at White House Farm. The Story of Jeremy Bamber*. Headline.

Jessel, D, Dr Blake, S, Morton, J & Waddell, B 1990: *Murder Casebook: The White House Farm Murders*. Marshall Cavendish.

Campbell, D, Wilson, C & Dr Persaud, R. 1996: *Murder in Mind: Jeremy Bamber*. Marshall Cavendish.

Wilkes, R. 1994: *Blood Relations*. Little Brown.

Websites

Attwood, S., 2021: White House Farm Murders https://www.youtube.com/watch?v=fEf2WCKkT1M&t=607s (accessed November 2024).

Criminal Cases Review Commission https://ccrc.gov.uk/decision/bamber-jeremy/ (accessed September 2024),

JBIC Ltd

https://www.jeremy-bamber.co.uk (accessed November 2021 – May 2025)

Jeremy Bamber Forum

https://jeremybamberforum.co.uk/index.php (accessed November 2021 – May 2025).

Osea Leisure
https://osealeisure.com/ (accessed January 2025)
Oxford English Dictionary
https://www.oed.com (accessed February 2025)
Oxford Reference
https://www.oxfordreference.com/display/10.1093/acref/9780199594009.001.0001/acref-9780199594009-e-0099 (accessed February 2025)
Peter Tatchell Foundation
https://www.petertatchellfoundation.org (accessed May 2025)
Poulton, S.
https://www.soniapoulton.co.uk/ (accessed January 2025)
Reddit
https://www.reddit.com (accessed November 2021-February 2025)
UK Justice Forum https://miscarriageofjustice.co/index.php?board=6.0 (accessed November 2021 – May 2025)
UK Parliament
https://www.parliament.uk/ (accessed April 2025)
Vaulty Manor
https://www.vaultymanor.co.uk (accessed September 2024)

Documentaries and Films

Banijay Crime, 2024: *Murders at White House Farm – Behind Mansion Walls.* YouTube.
Bleksley, P. 2024: *Crime Suspect.* Talk TV.
Gammon, L, 2021: *The Bambers – Murder at the Farm.* Mindhouse Productions.
Mole, C. 2020: *Faking It: Tears of a Crime, Jeremy Bamber.* RDF Television.
Perks, J. & Le Han, M. 2011: *Crimes that Shook Britain.* Title Role Productions.
Vile, J & Wood, E, 2020: *The Ripper.* Netflix.
Whittington, P, 2020: *White House Farm.* New Pictures
Williams-Thomas, M, 2012: *Bamber – The New Evidence.* ITV.

Podcasts

DiNino, A. 2024: *Crime Bistro, The Murders at White House Farm.*

JBIC Ltd, 2022: *Jeremy Bamber and White House Farm* (Various Episodes).

Maguire, H. & Bala, S. 2020: *White House Farm Revisited – The Contested Evidence.*

Pacheco, L. 2024: *The Murders at White House Farm Podcast, HBO Max.*

Page, K. 2023: *The White House Farm Murders (Various Episodes).*

Online Articles

Allison, E. 2011: *Jeremy Bamber: I will feel hope again* https://www.theguardian.com/uk/audio/2011/jan/30/jeremy-bamber-murder-appeal-audio?intcmp=239

Blake, H. 2024: *Did the U.K.'s Most Infamous Family Massacre End in a Wrongful Conviction?* https://www.newyorker.com/magazine/2024/08/05/did-the-uks-most-infamous-family-massacre-end-in-a-wrongful-conviction

Hattenstone, S. & Taylor, D. 2020: *Jeremy Bamber refused access to documents on family murders* https://www.theguardian.com/uk-news/2020/jun/05/jeremy-bamber-refused-access-to-documents-on-essex-family-murders

Hattenstone, S. 2025: Review body CCRC refuses to refer Jeremy Bamber murder case back to court of appeal https://www.theguardian.com/uk-news/2025/jul/04/review-body-ccrc-refuses-to-refer-jeremy-bamber-murder-case-back-court-of-appeal

Jones, S. 2025: *D-Day for Killer Jeremy Bamber* https://www.dailymail.co.uk/news/article-14376721/killer-Jeremy-Bamber-White-House-Farm-murders.html (accessed April 2025)

Mercer, D. 2021: *Louis Theroux examines Jeremy Bamber murders – and reveals why 'legit' people believe five-time killer is innocent*

https://news.sky.com/story/louis-theroux-examines-jeremy-bamber-murders-and-reveals-why-legit-people-believe-five-time-killer-is-innocent-12406985

Morse, F. 2013: *The Sun newspaper's '1,200 killed by mental patients' headline labelled 'irresponsible and wrong'* https://www.independent.co.uk/news/uk/the-sun-newspaper-s-1-200-killed-by-mental-patients-headline-labelled-irresponsible-and-wrong-8863893.html

Pidd, H. & Topping, A. 2020: *'It was toxic': how sexism threw police off the trail of the Yorkshire Ripper* https://www.theguardian.com/uk-news/2020/nov/13/it-was-toxic-how-sexism-threw-police-off-the-trail-of-the-yorkshire-ripper

Press Association, 2010: *Farm killer Jeremy Bamber reveals 'new evidence' in bid to clear name* https://www.independent.co.uk/news/uk/crime/farm-killer-jeremy-bamber-reveals-new-evidence-in-bid-to-clear-name-2044316.html

Original Interviews

Bone, A. January 2025

Page, K. February 2025

Roberts, N. January 2025

Eady, Dr D. February 2025

Personal Correspondence

Bamber, J. 2021-2025 Letters to author

Walker, P. 2025 Email to author

Notes

Two Sides of the Same Coin

1. Caffell, 1995
2. Caffell, 1995
3. Caffell, 1995
4. Gammon, 2021
5. Lee, 2016
6. Page, 2023
7. Lee, 2016

White House Farm

1. Osea Leisure 2025

Phyllis and Jeremy

1. Lee, 2016
2. Caffell, 1995
3. Lee, 2016
4. Lee, 2016
5. Caffell, 1995
6. Lee, 2016
7. Gammon, 2021
8. Lee, 2016
9. Lee, 2016

The Devil's Child

1. Caffell, 1995
2. Gammon, 2021
3. Caffell, 1995

4. Lee, 2016
5. Caffell, 1995
6. Lee, 2016
7. Lee, 2016
8. Lee, 2016
9. Lee, 2016
10. Lee, 2016
11. Caffell, 1995

Turmoil

1. Gammon, 2021
2. Lee, 2016
3. Gammon, 2021
4. Lee, 2016
5. Lee, 2016
6. Lee, 2016
7. Lee, 2016

I didn't mean to be horrible to Jeremy

1. Caffell, 1995
2. Caffell, 1995
3. Lee, 2016
4. Lee, 2016
5. Caffell, 1995
6. Caffell, 1995
7. Caffell, 1995
8. Lee, 2016
9. Lee, 2016
10. Lee, 2016
11. Lee, 2016
12. Lee, 2016
13. Lee, 2016
14. Lee, 2016

15. Lee, 2016
16. Lee, 2016
17. Gammon, 2021

Oh God, I hope she hasn't done anything silly

1. UK Justice Forum
2. Lee, 2016
3. Lee, 2016
4. UK Justice Forum
5. UK Justice Forum
6. Lee, 2016
7. Lee, 2016
8. Lee, 2016
9. Lee, 2016
10. Lee, 2016
11. Lee, 2016
12. Lee, 2016
13. Lee, 2016
14. Lee, 2016
15. UK Justice Forum

Five Dead in Total

1. Lee, 2016
2. UK Justice Forum
3. UK Justice Forum
4. UK Justice Forum
5. UK Justice Forum
6. UK Justice Forum
7. UK Justice Forum
8. UK Justice Forum
9. UK Justice Forum
10. UK Justice Forum
11. UK Justice Forum

Jeremy, both your parents are dead

1. Lee, 2016
2. Gammon, 2021
3. Lee, 2016
4. Lee, 2016
5. Lee, 2016
6. Lee, 2016
7. UK Justice Forum
8. UK Justice Forum
9. UK Justice Forum
10. UK Justice Forum
11. Lee, 2016
12. Lee, 2016
13. Lee, 2016
14. Lee, 2016
15. Lee, 2016
16. UK Justice Forum
17. Lee, 2016
18. Lee, 2016
19. Lee, 2016
20. Lee, 2016
21. Lee, 2016
22. UK Justice Forum
23. Lee, 2016
24. Lee, 2016
25. Lee, 2016

Long Shapely Legs

1. Caffell, 1995
2. Press Association
3. Caffell, 1995
4. Caffell, 1995
5. Caffell, 1995

6. Caffell, 1995
7. Vile, 2020
8. Caffell, 1995

The Boss

1. Lee, 2016
2. Caffell, 1995
3. Caffell, 1995
4. Lee, 2016
5. Lee, 2016
6. Lee, 2016
7. Lee, 2016
8. Gammon, 2021
9. Lee, 2016
10. Lee, 2016
11. Lee, 2016
12. Gammon, 2021
13. Lee, 2016

Inheritance

1. Lee, 2016
2. Caffell, 1995
3. Caffell, 1995
4. Caffell, 1995
5. Caffell, 1995

Discoveries

1. Lee, 2016
2. Lee, 2016
3. Lee, 2016
4. Lee, 2016
5. Lee, 2016

Love Hurts

1. Lee, 2016
2. Lee, 2016
3. Lee, 2016
4. Lee, 2016
5. Lee, 2016
6. Lee, 2016
7. Lee, 2016
8. Lee, 2016
9. Lee, 2016
10. Lee, 2016
11. Lee, 2016

Mistakes Had Been Made

1. Gammon, 2021
2. Gammon, 2021
3. Gammon, 2021
4. Lee, 2016
5. UK Justice Forum
6. Caffell, 1995
7. Lee, 2016
8. Lee, 2016

I could kill anyone. I could even kill my parents.

1. Lee, 2016
2. UK Justice Forum
3. UK Justice Forum
4. UK Justice Forum
5. Oxford Reference
6. Lee, 2016
7. Lee, 2016
8. Lee, 2016
9. Lee, 2016
10. Lee, 2016

Do you believe Jeremy Bamber or do you believe Julie Mugford?

1. Lee, 2016
2. Lee, 2016
3. UK Justice Forum
4. Lee, 2016
5. Lee, 2016
6. Lee, 2016
7. Lee, 2016
8. Lee, 2016

Matters of Pure Speculation

1. Lee, 2016
2. Lee, 2016
3. Lee, 2016
4. Wilkes, 1994
5. Lee, 2016
6. Lee, 2016
7. CCRC 2025
8. Lee, 2016

She's got hold of one of my guns

1. UK Justice Forum
2. UK Justice Forum
3. Page, 2023
4. Harrison, 2015
5. JBIC Ltd
6. Roberts, 2025
7. UK Justice Forum
8. UK Justice Forum
9. Blake, 2024
10. Blake, 2024
11. UK Justice Forum

12. Bone, 2025
13. UK Justice Forum
14. JBIC Ltd
15. Harrison, 2015
16. UK Justice Forum
17. JBIC Ltd
18. UK Justice Forum
19. JBIC Ltd, 2022
20. JBIC Ltd
21. JBIC Ltd
22. Walker, 2025
23. Walker, 2025
24. JBIC Ltd
25. Page, 2023
26. Hattenstone, 2025
27. Hattenstone, 2025

The Tragedies

1. CCRC
2. JBIC Ltd
3. Eady, 2025
4. JBIC Ltd
5. JBIC Ltd
6. Page, 2023
7. Page, 2023
8. Page, 2023
9. Page, 2023
10. Walker, 2025
11. JBIC Ltd, 2022
12. JBIC Ltd, 2022
13. Walker, 2025
14. JBIC Ltd, 2022
15. JBIC Ltd, 2022
16. JBIC Ltd, 2022
17. JBIC Ltd, 2022

18. JBIC Ltd, 2022
19. Page, 2023
20. Page, 2023
21. JBIC Ltd, 2022
22. Walker, 2025
23. JBIC Ltd
24. JBIC Ltd, 2022
25. JBIC Ltd, 2022
26. Eady, 2025
27. JBIC Ltd, 2022
28. JBIC Ltd, 2022
29. Gammon, 2021

Mental Gymnastics

1 Oxford English Dictionary
2 Jeremy Bamber Forum
3 UK Justice Forum
4 UK Justice Forum
5 Jeremy Bamber Forum
6 Jeremy Bamber Forum
7 Peter Tatchell Foundation
8 Peter Tatchell Foundation
9 Banijay Crime, 2024
10 UK Parliament 2022
11 Sonia Poulton
12 Bleksley, 2024
13 Page, 2025
14 Page, 2025
15 Mercer, 2021
16 Mercer, 2021

Stranger Things Have Happened

1. Foot, 1975
2. Foot, 1975
3. Foot, 1975

4. Foot, 1975
5. Foot, 1975
6. Foot, 1975
7. Foot, 1975
8. Foot, 1975
9. Banijay Crime, 2024
10. Crispin, 1987
11. Crispin, 1987
12. Crispin, 1987
13. Reddit, 2021

A Life of Less Liberty

1. Mole, 2020
2. Jeremy Bamber Forum
3. Bamber, 2021